20th CENTURY JEWELRY & THE ICONS OF STYLE

STEFANO PAPI & ALEXANDRA RHODES

20th CENTURY JEWELRY & THE ICONS OF STYLE

REVISED EDITION

WITH 475 ILLUSTRATIONS
IN COLOUR AND BLACK AND WHITE

Thames & Hudson

In loving memory of Alexandra

STEFANO PAPI has worked as Senior European Specialist in the jewelry departments of both Sotheby's and Christie's. His books include *Stage Jewels* and *Jewels of the Romanovs*, and he is co-author, with Alexandra Rhodes, of *Famous Jewelry Collectors*.

ALEXANDRA RHODES, a Fellow of the Gemmological Association of Great Britain, was Senior Director of Sotheby's and a Senior International Specialist of the jewelry department, based in London. She is also co-author, with Stefano Papi, of *Famous Jewelry Collectors*.

Front cover: Cecil Beaton, *Maria Callas*, 1957 (see p. 209). Photo courtesy of the Cecil Beaton Studio Archive, Sotheby's.

Back cover: A gem-set butterfly brooch, probably by Boivin and designed by Suzanne Belperron, mid-1930s (see p. 116). Private collection.

Frontispiece: A necklace from the collection of Daisy Fellowes. Designed to resemble a waterfall, it is set with circular-cut diamonds and seven cabochon emerald drops (see pp. 102–3).

First published in the United Kingdom in 2013 by Thames & Hudson Ltd, 181A High Holborn, London WC1V 7QX

This revised edition 2016

20th Century Jewelry and the Icons of Style © 2013 and 2016 Stefano Papi and Alexandra Rhodes

Designed by Turchini Design Ltd, London

British Library Cataloguing-in-Publication Data A catalogue record for this book is available from the British Library

ISBN 978-0-500-51900-4

Printed and bound in China by Toppan Leefung Printing Limited

To find out about all our publications, please visit **www.thamesandhudson.com**. There you can subscribe to our e-newsletter, browse or download our current catalogue, and buy any titles that are in print.

Contents

Preface

An object of beauty and desire, a jewel also provides a perfect reflection of the personality, lifestyle and tastes of the owner. Jewelry auctions are not a new phenomenon, but over the past few decades a wealth of the world's most fabulous jewels, once belonging to some of the most notable personalities of the 20th century, have passed through the salerooms. These jewels were formerly in the possession of members of royalty, the aristocracy, high society and stars of the screen. In each instance, whether one item or a whole collection, the pieces of jewelry offer us a fascinating insight into the life and times of the owner as well as the opportunity to see some of the finest gemstones and the most stunning jewels ever created.

The 'Roaring Twenties' saw the birth of a glittering social scene after the darkness of the First World War. Drastic changes in Europe had put an end to several monarchies, and powerful figures from the world of business now rose to join the social elite. The jewels that had once adorned the empresses and queens of old royal families passed into new hands. Women, more independent and influential than ever before, broke with the restrictive customs of the past: they cut their hair, abandoned their corsets and wore looser-fitting clothes. This change in fashion led to a new style of jewelry, reaching a high point in 1925 at the Exposition des Arts Décoratifs in Paris; historic gemstones were reset and new jewels were created.

This was a glamorous period for such rich and powerful society women as those described in this book, leading hectic, international lives for which they required designer dresses and designer jewels. They included Ganna Walska, heiresses such as Marjorie Merriweather Post and Barbara Hutton, film stars such as Merle Oberon and aristocrats such as Daisy Fellowes. For the discerning collectors who graced the social scene in the 1920s and 1930s, their jewelry was not only an accessory or statement of social standing, but also had an irresistible attraction that went beyond its intrinsic value. They could afford to buy the best, and with their great sense of style built unique and memorable collections, often with the help of the jewels' skilled and imaginative creators.

A major figure in the beau monde of the 1930s was the Duchess of Windsor, who built up an incomparable jewelry collection over the years. These pieces were not only some of the most important and sensational examples of the 20th-century jeweler's art, but also the jewels chosen by a king to give to the woman for whom he abdicated his throne.

The work of French jewelers was the most in-demand in the international high society in which these women moved, with the historic firms of Chaumet and Boucheron maintaining the outstanding reputations they had held at the turn of the century. Cartier, called by Edward VII when he was Prince of Wales 'the King of Jewelers, Jewelers to Kings', was still pre-eminent. Van Cleef & Arpels, founded in 1906, became one of the most fashionable jewelers of the inter-war years, and innovative creations by the firm of Boivin and the designer Suzanne Belperron were essential elements in every stylish woman's collection.

Following the turmoil and tragedy of the Second World War, high society started to flourish again, as did the fashion houses and the jewelry business. New Yorker Harry Winston, who had first opened his doors in 1932, became the most sought-after jeweler for extraordinary stones, especially diamonds. The well-known figures of the pre-war years were now joined by women such as the Maharani of Baroda, the Begum Aga Khan and Nina Dyer, each of whom created a stunning jewelry collection. The 1950s also saw the emergence of the legendary opera star Maria Callas, known as 'La Divina', and Hélène Rochas, an enduring icon of beauty and elegance.

The collections formed by these women consisted of some of the most beautiful and extravagant jewels ever made and provide a fascinating insight into the intriguing personalities and worlds of their owners.

STEFANO PAPI & ALEXANDRA RHODES

Marjorie Merriweather Post

1

The Hillwood Museum in Washington, DC, is the setting for one of the most magnificent collections of precious objects from Tsarist Russia and a splendid display of French decorative art. Its creator was Marjorie Merriweather Post, who left her house and its treasures for the benefit of future generations when she died in 1973. Wandering through the mansion and beautiful gardens of the 25-acre estate, one can still feel the allure of this grande dame of a bygone era.

Marjorie was born on 15 March 1887 in Springfield, Illinois, the only daughter of Charles William Post, owner of the Postum Cereal Company, and Ella Letitia Merriweather. At the age of 18 Marjorie married investment banker Edward Bennett Close, with whom she had two daughters, Adelaide and Eleanor. When her father died in 1914 she inherited a vast fortune and his company; she was just 27. Two years later her provincial lifestyle completely changed when the family moved to New York City. They lived in the Burden mansion on 5th Avenue, which Marjorie started to decorate with beautiful 18th-century French furniture, a style then in vogue with New York society. The connoisseur and art dealer Sir Joseph Duveen helped to educate her taste and she developed an interest in decorative art, including *objets de vertu*.

In 1919, Marjorie's marriage to Close ended and a year later she married the financier Edward Francis Hutton, who became chairman of the board of the Postum Cereal Company in 1923. It was probably that year in which she received a sapphire and diamond bracelet made by Cartier, set at the centre with a magnificent cushion-shaped 58.33 cts sapphire from the famous mines of Kashmir (p. 14). These stones are the most sought after and valuable sapphires in the world, thanks to their unrivalled velvety blue colour. It is very rare to find a sapphire of this origin exceeding 20 cts, so Marjorie's stone is truly exceptional. A photograph of Marjorie from 1921 shows her wearing on her hat a long brooch of epaulette design, terminating with a pearl and a coloured stone, indicating her taste for the latest fashion; it is very similar to one created by Cartier in 1914 and elongated in the 1920s (p. 8).

Hutton was a skilled businessman and he developed the Postum Cereal Company by acquiring a number of other food brands, including Birdseye, and in 1929 the firm became the General Foods Corporation. The couple enjoyed the glamorous social scene of the 1920s and Marjorie hosted charity events in their many properties, including houses on the north shore of Long Island and at Palm Beach. In 1924, in a move that was common at the time, she decided to sell her New York mansion to the George F. Fuller construction company, which wanted to build an apartment block on the site. Marjorie agreed but only on condition that they build a triplex apartment with a separate ground-floor concierge, parking and entrance so that she could maintain her address on East 92nd Street while the other residents entered on Fifth Avenue. The apartment was the largest in New York with 54 rooms and 17 bathrooms; everything was created to the highest standards of the period. The panelled dining room could accommodate 125 people.

During this period Marjorie further refined her taste, not only for French porcelain and furniture but also for magnificent jewelry to suit her high-society lifestyle. Like every important lady of that time, she loved to wear long strings of pearls, as depicted in Frank O. Salisbury's 1931 portrait of her (p. 17), and throughout her life she often wore two strings of beautiful natural pearls graduating in size. Most of her jewelry from this era has been unmounted and redesigned in more contemporary settings to suit changing fashions. Some, however, has survived, such as a diamond tiara created by Cartier in a geometric pattern typical of the time and set at the centre with a step-cut diamond of 13.38 cts (p. 14); a diamond and *calibré*-cut ruby strap bracelet (p. 16) – a very elegant example of this period – as well as important diamond and emerald single-stone rings.

One of the most spectacular jewels in Marjorie's collection dates from these years: an emerald and diamond *sautoir* by Cartier, London, created in 1928–29. The long necklace was later shortened (p. 12) to a line of 24 tumbled emerald drops, each one surmounted by an emerald bead and interspersed with a barrel-shaped motif pavé-set with diamonds. Originally, it had a pendant set with an engraved emerald of 47.20 cts in a lyre-shaped diamond motif, but that was reused later in the year by Cartier as a centrepiece in a diamond bandeau. To replace the pendant, a buckle-shaped motif that supports a cascade of pear-shaped emeralds was added (right). It was designed by the London branch of Cartier in 1923 and set at its centre is a large emerald carved with a 17th-century Mughal motif of a flower, bearing on the side a Persian inscription that translates as 'The Servant of Shah Abbas'. In 1929, at Marjorie's request, the buckle-shaped motif was altered by Cartier, New York, so that it could also be used as a brooch. Later that year, Giulio de Blass depicted it in this form on Marjorie's shoulder in his painting of her with her daughter Nedenia Hutton, who had been born in 1923. Marjorie wore the full version of the *sautoir* to great effect at the Everglades Ball in Palm Beach in 1929, when she was dressed as Juliette (p. 11).

As well as the most elegant creations of the 1920s, Marjorie's collection became rich with beautiful stones and historic pieces. In June 1929, she was presented at court in London. She wore a pair of pendent earrings with two pear-shaped diamonds, weighing 14.25 and 20.34 cts respectively. Cartier had acquired them in 1928 from the collection of the Russian Prince Felix Yusupov, who said that they had belonged to Marie Antoinette, Queen of France. Cartier then sold the pair to Marjorie, with each of the two historic stones now hanging from a triangular-shaped diamond. Marjorie's elegant gown was enhanced by the addition of a diamond *devant de corsage* from the early 20th century, which she used as her left shoulder strap (p. 15).

Page 8
Marjorie Merriweather Post photographed in 1921. On her hat is a brooch of epaulette design similar to the one illustrated below, which was created by Cartier in 1914 and altered in 1920, set with diamonds, onyx, pearl, ruby and tourmaline.

Above
An emerald and diamond pendant by Cartier. In the photograph opposite, taken on the occasion of the Everglades Ball in 1929, Marjorie, dressed as Juliette, is wearing the pendant with an emerald and diamond *sautoir* (long necklace).

The year 1929 was a period of great achievement and happiness for Marjorie, but the euphoric roaring 1920s came to an end on Tuesday 29 October with the Wall Street Crash. Marjorie was not affected in the same way as others because General Foods continued to make a profit, but she was a sensitive and down-to-earth woman who realized that a glamorous lifestyle was not appropriate in a period of depression. Instead, she began to devote her time and energy to helping victims of the financial crisis. She put her jewelry collection in a safety-deposit box and with the money that she saved on the insurance she set up the Marjorie Post Hutton Canteen to help women and children in New York; her husband created the Edward F. Hutton Food Station for Men. Marjorie also established a delivery service for the elderly and the sick so that they did not have to make the trip downtown to pick up their food, and she dedicated time to organizing events to raise money for this and other charitable causes. Her good works extended to an anti-crime campaign, for which she was awarded the Cross of Honor from the United States Flag Association by the incoming first lady Eleanor Roosevelt on 12 December 1932. In contrast, Marjorie's niece, the Woolworth heiress Barbara Hutton, continued to indulge in an expensive lifestyle throughout these difficult times. This deeply upset her discreet and empathetic aunt.

After sixteen years, the marriage between Marjorie and Edward F. Hutton fell apart because of his philandering. In February 1935, when she was planning divorce proceedings, she met the man who was to become her third husband: Joseph E. Davies, a successful Washington attorney in corporate and international law. At the time of their first encounter, at a friend's dinner party in Palm Beach, they were both married – but this did not prevent them from falling in love. When their relationship took a serious turn, Joseph, like Marjorie, sought a divorce. Finally, on 15 December 1935, the couple married. Even though the press was not present, reports said that she was elegantly dressed in a beautiful pink gown, with the wedding cake and its flower decoration matching the hue of her dress. After the ceremony, the couple boarded Marjorie's

The emerald and diamond *sautoir* created in 1928–29 by Cartier, London, was later made into a shorter necklace, at Marjorie's request.

yacht, *Hussar V* – rechristened *Sea Cloud* to celebrate the marriage – for a honeymoon cruise in the West Indies. When it was launched in 1931, this vessel was listed in the *Guinness Book of Records* as being the world's largest privately owned sailing yacht: from stern to bow it measured 96.32 metres, with 16,764 metres of sail and a complement of 72 crew. It was a real castle on the sea, with lavishly decorated interiors, including a bedroom with Louis XVI furniture and a pink marble bathroom, a cinema for entertainment on long journeys and even a fully equipped operating theatre with a team of doctors, in case of an emergency.

Once back from her trip, Marjorie became a member of the Board of Directors at General Foods; her appointment as the company's first ever female director was announced in April 1936. That August, President Franklin D. Roosevelt appointed her husband American Ambassador to the Soviet Union, with the delicate task of fostering a good relationship between Russia and the United States at a time when the policies of Nazi Germany – the Rhineland had been occupied in March – had increased international tension. Marjorie was at first appalled at the prospect of going to Moscow, but she threw herself into organizing their move and knew she could help her husband charm the Russians.

She left most of her legendary jewels in a safe in the United States, but she did instruct Cartier, New York, to combine two existing diamond and sapphire bracelets to form a necklace. The final creation was quite spectacular, with the focus in the centre where a diamond and sapphire motif was created using a large cushion-shaped sapphire (p. 19). The motif can be detached and used as a brooch. In 1946, Salisbury painted Marjorie wearing the necklace (p. 18).

The couple arrived in Moscow on 19 January 1937. Living in the Soviet Union was not easy: Marjorie's phone calls were often intercepted and in this period of the purges Soviet officials would mysteriously disappear. Amid the turmoil, exquisite works of art from the Tsarist era came onto the market and this gave Marjorie a unique opportunity. Prior to her arrival, she owned only two Russian items: a box – her first Fabergé piece – from the Yusupov collection, which she had bought from Cartier in 1920, and the Catherine the Great Easter Egg, also by Fabergé, that Tsar Nicholas II had presented to his mother, the

Dowager Empress Maria Feodorovna, for Easter in 1914. This was given to Marjorie by her daughter Eleanor in 1931. In Moscow, the Soviet government was selling art in order to raise money for its industrialization projects, and it paid little attention to the historical value of the items sold. Marjorie, with her collector's instinct and eye for beauty, took the chance to acquire a wide variety of items, from paintings and furniture to porcelain and icons. Fortunately, Joe Davies shared her passion for collecting. Objects were stacked in dust-covered piles in warehouses and she excitedly rummaged through them, buying as much as she could. The eighteen months that Marjorie spent in the Soviet Union sparked an interest in Russian art that was to continue for the rest of her life; many of the pieces of Tsarist art that came out of Russia after the Revolution eventually found their way into her collection from dealers worldwide. Ultimately she possessed the most comprehensive collection of Russian Imperial art outside of Russia.

A sapphire and diamond bracelet by Cartier, c. 1923. At the centre is a cushion-shaped sapphire of 58.33 cts from Kashmir. The sapphire can be detached and Harry Winston later made a diamond mount so that it could be worn as a ring.

A diamond tiara made by Cartier for Marjorie in the early 1930s. At the centre it is set with a step-cut diamond weighing 13.38 cts.

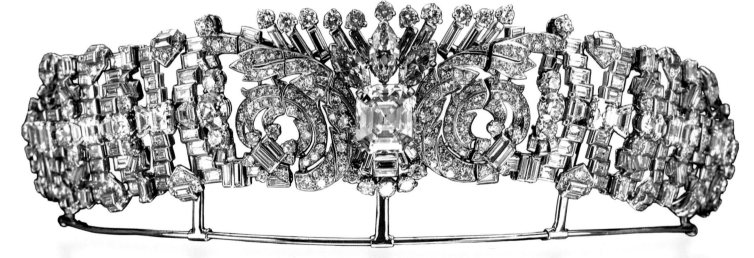

Top
The Marie Antoinette diamond earrings. The two pear-shaped diamonds weighing 14.25 and 20.34 cts respectively were mounted by Cartier in 1928. They came from the collection of Prince Felix Yusupov but reputedly had once belonged to Marie Antoinette, Queen of France. They are now in the Smithsonian.

Above
An emerald and diamond ring by the American jeweler Harry Winston, 1950s.

Right
Marjorie dressed for her presentation at court in 1929, painted by Giulio de Blaas. She is wearing the Marie Antoinette diamond earrings.

In June 1938, the Davieses completed their mission in Russia and the government presented Marjorie with a pair of antique vases that she was allowed to choose for herself as a leaving gift. In July, Joe was appointed Ambassador to both Belgium and the Grand Duchy of Luxembourg. The couple took up residence in Brussels in the Palais du Marquis d'Assche, at one time home to members of the royal family and birthplace of the reigning King Léopold III. The 19th-century house was still being renovated when they arrived and Marjorie made great efforts to decorate it appropriately. From her residence in New York she brought her François Boucher tapestries, French furniture and Russian porcelain. She was delighted to be in a country with a monarchy and Joe soon established good relations with the King. Marjorie was in her element amid the grandeur and rituals of the Belgian royal court.

While they were in Brussels, Marjorie, Joe and Nedenia listened with increasing alarm to Hitler's speeches on the radio: Europe was on the brink of war. At the time of the Munich crisis at the end of September, Joe was so worried that he sent Marjorie and Nedenia back to the safety of the United States. Marjorie returned in mid-November, since Hitler had been temporarily placated by the annexation of the Sudetenland. On 14 December 1938, she held her first diplomatic dinner in Brussels and proved herself to be the perfect hostess. The food was served on the Russian service for the Order of St George, to great effect.

The peace did not last, however. The Nazis' invasion of Poland on 1 September 1939 led England and France to declare war on Germany. The Davieses were on vacation in the United States at the time and the Department of State forbade the ambassador's family from going back to Europe – even to pick up its personal possessions. Nonetheless, the resourceful Marjorie sent several assistants to Brussels to collect her belongings and transport them back to the United States before the situation deteriorated further.

Davies resigned from his post in Belgium and, to Marjorie's relief, returned home. Back in Washington, he acted as an intermediary between the United States and Europe in his role as special assistant to the Secretary of State, Cordell Hull. The Davieses started to look for a permanent residence and, after some months, found a neo-Georgian house with 20 acres of land in northwest Washington that had once belonged to the wife of Alexander Graham Bell. With her design flair, Marjorie made extensive changes to the interior of the property to display her collections to advantage and brought everything from the triplex in New York, which she now gave up. Marjorie gave Joe ownership of the estate, to save his pride, and in 1942 when the family finally moved in it was renamed Tregaron after the Welsh village that his family came from.

On 7 December 1941, the United States was brought into the war by the surprise attack on Pearl Harbor by the Japanese. Marjorie, with her enormous generosity and sense of civic responsibility, leased the *Sea Cloud*, stripped of its fixtures and fittings, to the US Navy for the token amount of $1 a year. It was used as a weather ship in the North Atlantic until 1944. Her characteristic kindness extended to the Grand Ducal family of Luxembourg – she gave them use of a house

A bracelet set with *calibré*-cut rubies and circular-cut and baguette diamonds, *c.* 1930.

Marjorie portrayed by Frank O. Salisbury in 1931. She is wearing pearl and ruby jewels and a ruby and diamond bracelet.

Marjorie, in a portrait by Frank
O. Salisbury, 1946, wearing the
sapphire and diamond necklace
(opposite) created for her in 1936
by Cartier using two existing
bracelets.

Below
A sapphire and diamond
ring set with an hexagonal step-
cut sapphire weighing 70.19 cts.

on her Long Island estate when they had to flee Europe
in 1940. She devoted her time to helping the war effort
through the American Red Cross and she and Joe
continued to be involved in Soviet–American affairs;
they hosted a meeting at Tregaron in 1942 to encour-
age better relations between officials of the two nations.
One room in the house was decorated with major pieces
from Marjorie's Russian collection. In May 1943, Joe,
despite declining health, went on one last diplomatic
mission to Moscow to meet with Stalin. In the same
year, Warner Brothers released a film of his bestselling
book *Mission to Moscow* (1941), starring Walter Huston
and Ann Harding as Joe and Marjorie. The film's posi-
tive depiction of life in the Soviet Union under Stalin
later drew criticism in the McCarthy era.

It was also at this time that Marjorie met Princess
Julia Cantacuzène through the Sulgrave Club, an
exclusive women's club for the Washington elite, of
which Marjorie had been a member since 1940. Inspired
by the Russian relief programme to help refugees that
the Princess had established after 1917, Marjorie displayed her magnificent Imperial Russian objects in an
exhibition in Manhattan to assist Russian war relief.
She loved to use her collection for the benefit of others.

After the Potsdam Conference in 1945, where he
was special advisor to President Harry Truman and
Secretary of State James F. Byrnes with the rank of
ambassador, Davies's political influence waned. With
the onset of the Cold War, his views on the importance
of co-operation with the Soviet Union were no longer
welcome. Ill and disillusioned, his relationship with
Marjorie also started to crumble.

After its war service, the *Sea Cloud* was returned
to Marjorie, together with $175,000 for its renovation.

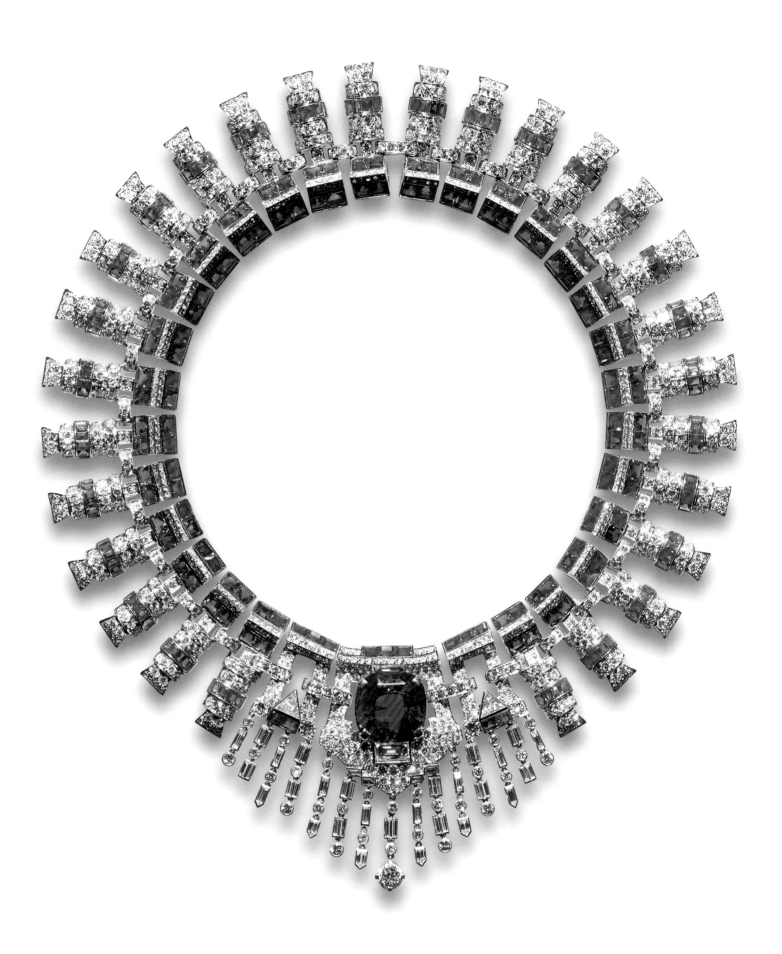

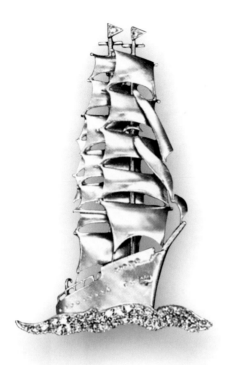

A platinum and diamond brooch in the form of Marjorie's yacht, the *Sea Cloud*.

Marjorie with her husband, Joe Davies, the Duke and Duchess of Windsor and friends on board the *Sea Cloud* in 1948.

Opposite
Marjorie with her daughter Eleanor and granddaughter Marwee.

She took great pride in restoring it to its former glory, which took nearly two years, and in April 1947 the family was finally able to set sail for the West Indies on a holiday. In the postwar years Joe was increasingly moody and possessive but Marjorie was determined to save the marriage and kept her unhappiness to herself. She concentrated on charity work and socializing, to take her mind off her personal troubles.

After Nedenia's marriage to Stanley M. Rumbough, Jr., an heir to the Colgate fortune, in 1946, the family rarely visited Hillwood, the mock-Tudor house and 122-acre estate on Long Island's Gold Coast, and Marjorie decided it was time to sell it. As it happened, this was just when Long Island University was seeking to expand and Hillwood, with its swimming pool and fields that could be used for sports and new buildings, was perfect for a campus. In June 1947, the university signed a contract to buy the estate for $200,000. But the local residents were afraid that hoardes of middle- and working-class students and minorities would be attracted to the new college and destroy the area's character. The Oyster Bay zoning board decided that the matter should be publicly discussed and on 10 July over 1,000 people turned up to express their concerns

at an impassioned meeting that lasted several hours. Protestors found issues and loopholes that kept the argument raging for four years. Marjorie declined to comment on the situation to the press, but behind the scenes she made sure that her financial managers and attorneys fought hard, and successfully, for Long Island University. True to her generous character, she thought it more important to provide a good education to future generations than to pander to local snobbery.

In 1948, Marjorie helped the Good Samaritan Hospital in Palm Beach by acting as chairman of the Everglades Club's 'New Look Ball' at which a 'Chinese auction' raised $176,000. The Duchess of Windsor was a member of the board and shortly after the event she and the Duke were invited for a cruise on the *Sea Cloud*. They sailed to Nassau and Havana, a journey that was enjoyed enormously by the Windsors and established a bond between the stylish Wallis and Marjorie. She celebrated this successful year with a stunning pair of

diamond ear clips set with a fringe of briolette diamonds, made by Van Cleef & Arpels (p. 23).

Marjorie brought together the most important members of society, present and upcoming, at her splendid receptions and dinners. She was renowned for these, and for her aristocratic allure; she was always elegantly dressed and sparkling with her fantastic jewels. The first impression of Lady Bird Johnson, the future first lady, when she was invited for dinner, was that everything around Marjorie had a regal aura – and this never faded. Her famous garden parties had to be perfect, from the flowers down to the tiniest detail. She found great joy in giving, and everyone invited was treated as a guest of honour, regardless of social standing. Despite her erect figure and stately presence, she was an extremely charming and open person with a great sense of humour. She loved to tango and at Mar-a-Lago, her mansion in Palm Beach, she provided instructors for her guests to learn the latest dances.

The large clasp of this necklace is set with brilliant-cut and baguette diamonds mounted in platinum, and supports a long, graduated fringe of brilliant-cut diamonds. The clasp was created by Cartier in 1960 from an existing piece in Marjorie's collection. In the centre is a pair of diamond pendent ear clips by Van Cleef & Arpels, 1948, set with brilliant-cut, baguette and briolette diamonds.

Opposite
Marjorie inspecting the table settings prior to a formal dinner at Hillwood, Washington, DC, in October 1965. She is wearing her pearl and diamond Cartier necklace.

Opposite
An amethyst, turquoise and diamond necklace created for Marjorie by Cartier in 1950 and matching ear clips with suspended fringes of briolette amethysts.

Left
Lady Bird Johnson with Marjorie at Mar-a-Lago, Palm Beach, in April 1968. Marjorie is wearing the Cartier amethyst, turquoise and diamond necklace.

Marjorie became famous for her square dances, where everyone dressed in Western costume, although her own outfit was always enhanced by her striking jewels, such as the set created for her by Cartier in 1950 in amethyst, turquoise and diamonds (p. 24), a combination of stones and colours made famous years earlier by the Duchess of Windsor.

Marjorie was always interested in all forms of the arts. In Washington, she encouraged and supported organizations and events that enhanced the cultural life of the nation's capital. In 1950, she started to take an interest in the National Symphony Orchestra and held a garden party to raise money for it. There she made friends with one of the orchestra's board members, Gerson Nordlinger, a cultured bachelor whom she was to invite to her parties frequently from that point onwards. Two years later, Nordlinger, as treasurer, held a meeting to discuss the orchestra's $90,000 deficit.

Marjorie took him aside and told him that she would pay off the whole debt. In 1954, when the orchestra had its first benefit ball, she acted as honorary chair. The following year, she donated $100,000 to fund a programme that would enable thousands of high-school students to attend National Symphony Orchestra concerts for free, giving many of them their first experience of live orchestral music. This benefited the NSO, too: its season was lengthened by five weeks, providing its players with more work and attracting better musicians. By the end of its first year, 500,000 students had participated in 'Music for Young America', as the programme was called, and it was a source of great pride to Marjorie. She loved to receive appreciative letters and comments from the teenagers who had benefited from her generosity.

Meanwhile, at home, Joe's temper grew shorter and his jealousy became unbearable. Marjorie, eleven years younger than her husband, was not even permitted to dance with another man without being questioned aggressively afterwards. In 1950, Joe was diagnosed with intestinal cancer and Marjorie felt duty-bound to remain with him. Once he had recovered, however, there was nothing to bind her to him but a piece of paper. When a friend, finding some documents relating to Marjorie's properties in 1954, asked why Tregaron had been bought in Joe's name, Marjorie pretended that this was news to her: the property, she claimed, was hers. Now with 'proof' that she had been severely wronged by her husband, she had an excuse to file for divorce. Joe, in his fury, refused to relinquish his claim on Tregaron. Unfortunately for Marjorie, the law was on his side. Their Russian art collection was divided in half and Joe ended up with objects that Marjorie had bought for herself using her own funds (she repurchased many of them after his death); in retaliation, a bitter and irate Marjorie sent a removal van to Tregaron

The 'Blue Heart' diamond ring, set with a fancy deep blue diamond of 30.62 cts, was bought by Marjorie from Harry Winston in 1964.

Below
The Duke of Windsor with the French ballet dancer Zizi Jeanmaire at a ball in aid of cancer research held in the orangerie at the Palace of Versailles, 16 June 1953. She wears the 'Blue Heart' mounted as a pendant with a blue and a pink diamond by Van Cleef & Arpels. This was the only time that the pendant was worn before being sold to Baron Thyssen-Bornemisza on 9 November 1953.

Above and below
A brilliant-cut diamond necklace by Harry Winston, *c.* 1965, and a 1950 diamond brooch by Cartier set with an articulated cascade of marquise-shaped diamonds.

Centre left
A ring by Harry Winston set with a cushion-shaped diamond of 31.20 cts. It is now known as the 'Merriweather Post' diamond.

Right
Marjorie attending the Red
Cross Ball in Palm Beach in 1968
wearing the ruby and diamond
necklace and pendent ear clips
illustrated opposite. The necklace,
of early 19th-century manufacture,
is set with oval-shaped rubies and
old-cut diamonds mounted in
silver and gold. The clips in the
matching pendent earrings were
a later addition.

Below
A late 19th-century brooch from
Marjorie's collection, designed as
a swooping hummingbird set with
rubies and diamonds.

in the dead of night to retrieve everything, from her celebrated azaleas to the mansion's oriental rugs. After a marriage of nearly twenty years, the divorce was finalized on 8 March 1955.

With the loss of Tregaron, Marjorie started to look for another property in Washington. On the edge of Rock Creek Park she found a neo-Georgian house called Arbremont with 25 acres of grounds, which she bought and renamed Hillwood after her former residence on Long Island. For some time she had envisaged giving her collection to the nation and for the next two years, with the help of the New York art dealers French & Company, she had the interiors of her new mansion remodelled to showcase her priceless artefacts. Hillwood became a treasure house of Imperial Russian art and 18th-century French furniture, as well as the setting for lectures given by the curator of her collection, Marvin Ross, who was hired in 1958.

Marjorie continued to acquire magnificent jewels, and in the late 1950s and early 1960s she made some important purchases through the jeweler Harry Winston. In 1960, she bought a 30.62 cts, heart-shaped fancy deep blue diamond. This stone had been mounted in the centre of a diamond corsage ornament by Cartier, Paris, in 1910, two years after it was discovered, and sold to Mrs Unzue, a wealthy Argentinian who owned it for forty-three years. In 1953, the three principal stones from this piece – the 'Blue Heart', a triangular blue diamond of 3.82 cts and a pear-shaped pink diamond of 2.05 cts – were set in clusters of diamonds

and hung from a diamond *rivière* necklace by Van Cleef & Arpels. It was worn in public only once – by the French ballet dancer Zizi Jeanmaire at a ball held on 16 June 1953 in the orangerie of the Palace of Versailles in aid of cancer research (p. 26) – before the pendant was sold on 9 November to Baron Hans Heinrich Thyssen-Bornemisza. He purchased it for his future wife, Nina Dyer, as a token of his love (see Chapter 11). Bought back by Van Cleef & Arpels in 1960, the 'Blue Heart' was later acquired by Harry Winston in 1964. He sold it to Marjorie mounted as a ring in a cluster of 25 brilliant-cut colourless diamonds with a total weight of 1.63 cts. In the same year she donated the priceless diamond to the Smithsonian Institution.

A few years earlier, Marjorie had bought another beautiful stone from Harry Winston: a cushion-shaped diamond of 31.20 cts, of the highest grade D colour, from the Golconda mines in India. This diamond was from the collection of Mae Rovensky, the wife of banker John E. Rovensky. She had achieved fame in 1916 when her then husband Morton F. Plant exchanged their house on Fifth Avenue and 52nd Street with Cartier for two strings of pearls worth over $1 million. Cartier, New York, is still located in that building. In January 1957, Winston had bought the stone at the sale of the late Mrs Rovensky's jewels and recut it from its original 31.40 cts before selling it to Marjorie. Today, it is known as the 'Merriweather Post' diamond (p. 27).

In 1958, Marjorie was married for the fourth and last time, to Herbert A. May, a member of the board of directors of the Wheeling and Lake Erie Railroad, and of the New York, Chicago and St Louis Railroad,

Marjorie at the Red Cross Ball in Palm Beach in 1967. She is wearing the turquoise and diamond Marie-Louise Diadem (opposite) and the necklace, earrings, bracelet, brooch and ring created by Harry Winston in 1961 to match it. The diadem, originally set with emeralds, was part of a *parure* given by Napoleon I to the Archduchess Marie-Louise of Austria on the occasion of their wedding. It was made in 1810 by Etienne Nitôt et Fils in Paris and is set in silver and gold with 1,006 old-cut diamonds weighing 700 cts. It was acquired by Van Cleef & Arpels in 1953 from a descendant of the Empress Marie-Louise; the firm later removed the emeralds and substituted them with turquoises and sold the diadem to Marjorie. In 1962, the diadem was displayed at the Louvre in Paris together with the original necklace, earrings and comb in an exhibition about the Empress. Marjorie donated the diadem to the Smithsonian Institution in Washington, DC, in 1971.

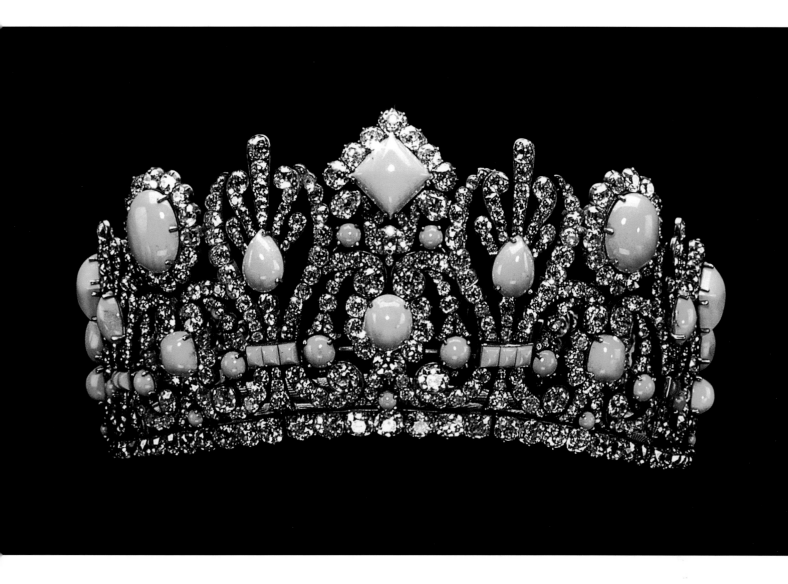

and an executive with Westinghouse Air Brake company. Her engagement ring was a navette-shaped diamond mounted horizontally. The marriage did not last long, however, and after six years the couple divorced. Marjorie was known thereafter by her maiden name.

In the year that marriage came to an end, 1964, Marjorie bought several pieces by Fabergé and another twenty or so over the next five years. These included the celebrated Music Box created by Fabergé to celebrate the twenty-fifth wedding anniversary of Princess Zinaida Yusupov and her husband, Felix, in 1907.

Marjorie also continued to add historic pieces to her jewelry collection. In 1960, she bought the Napoleon Diamond Necklace from Harry Winston, donating it two years later to the Smithsonian Institution. It is primarily composed of forty-seven old-cut, pear-shaped and briolette diamonds and has an estimated total weight of 263 cts. Mounted in gold topped with silver, the necklace was created in 1811 by the court jeweler Etienne Nitôt et Fils of Paris for Napoleon to give to his second wife, Marie-Louise, Empress of France, to celebrate the birth of their son, Napoleon II, the King of Rome. After the fall of Napoleon, Marie-Louise took the necklace back to Vienna with her other personal jewels and it remained in the Habsburg family until 1948, when it was sold to the French dealer from whom Winston acquired it.

The necklace was not the only piece of Marie-Louise's jewelry that Marjorie possessed. She owned an imposing diadem, also made by Etienne Nitôt et Fils, that Napoleon had presented to Marie-Louise on the occasion of their marriage in 1810. It was originally part of a set that included a necklace, earrings and a comb, all mounted with emeralds and diamonds. On

The turquoise and diamond necklace created by Harry Winston for Marjorie and which she wore with the Marie-Louise Diadem.

Opposite
Marjorie and guests in the French drawing room at Hillwood, Washington, DC, listening to a lecture on French furniture by the curator of her collection, Marvin Ross.

her death, Empress Marie-Louise bequeathed the set to her aunt, Archduchess Elise, whose descendant sold it in 1953 to Van Cleef & Arpels. The firm removed the emeralds from the diadem and sold them individually, mounted in pieces of jewelry. A newspaper advertisement for Van Cleef & Arpels in 1955 read, 'An emerald for you from the historic Napoleonic Tiara.' The diadem, now set with turquoises in place of the emeralds, was then sold to Marjorie (p. 33). Harry Winston created a turquoise and diamond necklace with matching pendent earrings, bracelet, brooch and ring that Marjorie wore with the Marie-Louise Diadem to the Red Cross Ball in Palm Beach in 1967. Oldric Royce designed a white and turquoise evening gown to complement the jewels (p. 32). In 1971, Marjorie gave the diadem to the Smithsonian.

Marjorie's jewelry collection also included modern pieces such as a stylish invisible setting ruby and diamond floral brooch made by Van Cleef & Arpels in 1967 and bought by her in 1969. Marjorie turned 80

that year and was making plans for the future of Hillwood and her collection. She proposed that on her death the entire house and collection would go to the Smithsonian Institution with an endowment to maintain it as a museum. This is what happened after Marjorie died of heart failure at Hillwood on 12 September 1973. However, the institution found it was too much of a financial burden, and the estate reverted to the Post Foundation in 1976. Finally, the property was opened to the public in 1977 as the Hillwood Estate, Museum and Gardens.

Marjorie's coat of arms had the Latin motto *Me Mea Spes Omnis*, meaning 'All my Hope is in Myself'. It encapsulated not only the self-sufficiency that she displayed through four not always happy marriages but also the philanthropy and capacity to improve the lives of others that was such a conspicuous part of her life of grandeur. That style of life has long gone but this elegant woman of unimaginable wealth left a legacy of refinement and education that lives on today. ✹

Lydia, Lady Deterding

2

On 20 November 1980, Christie's in Geneva held a sale of the magnificent jewelry collection of the late Lydia, Lady Deterding. At the front of the catalogue was a portrait by Philip de László of an elegant woman with an enigmatic smile who was as intriguing as the historically important pieces to be auctioned. In the absence of any biography, this painting offered a clue to her character and lifestyle; for although Lady Deterding was a familiar figure in international high society, little was known about her. Far more famous was her former husband, Sir Henri Deterding, a Dutchman whose highly successful career in the oil industry is well documented. Deterding played an instrumental role in the 1907 merger of Royal Dutch Petroleum with Shell Transport and Trading to form Royal Dutch Shell, and under his astute leadership the new company enjoyed extraordinary growth. For his services to Britain in the First World War he was given an honorary knighthood in 1920. He resigned from his position as director general of Shell at the age of 70 in 1936, at which point he was regarded as one of the most impressive entrepreneurs of the 20th century. His second wife, Lydia, however, has always been something of an enigma.

In conformity with the customs of her generation, Lydia kept the exact date of her birth a closely guarded secret, even from her immediate family. It is known that she was born Lydia Pavlovna Kudoyarov towards the end of the 19th century and that she was the daughter of the Tsarist general Pavel Kudoyarov. Her early life was spent in Tashkent (then capital of Russian Turkestan), thousands of kilometres from the fashionable European centres she would later inhabit. She never forgot her origins, however, and they may have been what instilled in her a strong appreciation of beautiful objects. At 16 Lydia married General Bagratouni, a Russian diplomat more than thirty years her senior. The first few years of their marriage were spent in St Petersburg, where they mixed in elite social circles. This was a time of pomp and grandeur in Imperial Russia, and it was bound to have nurtured Lydia's enthusiasm for gatherings at the highest level. Though she rarely talked about her past, Lydia did tell her two daughters from her second marriage about her encounters with members of the Russian Imperial family, as well as with the mysterious Rasputin, whom she had found 'terrifying'.

The couple soon left St Petersburg for Paris, where Bagratouni was appointed attaché. In the circles in which they moved, Lydia met Henri Deterding, again a much older man and a widower, who fell in love with her. By 1924 she was divorced and they married in London. They lived with their daughters, Lilla and Olga, in great style and comfort at Buckhurst Park in Ascot. Because of Deterding's enormous wealth and his constant anxiety lest his daughters be kidnapped for ransom, the family was surrounded by high security; yet the grounds at Buckhurst Park were so large that the two girls never felt unduly restricted. Their early years were spent in a happy and loving environment and they adored their 'Mama', who was affectionately described by one daughter as being not the 'perfect Mother in the true sense of the word' but nonetheless was an 'extraordinary person'.

Lady Deterding did not have what might be considered classical good looks, but she had a magnetic personality and de László's portrait captures the alluring sparkle in her eyes. She had an instinctive sense of style and adored the expensive trappings of life. Deterding, who was captivated by his new wife, showered her with costly jewels and designer clothes, knowing how much pleasure they gave her. Lydia's ease in international high society and her vivacity and animated conversation made her the ideal hostess for Henri's many guests. The sporting habits of the rich held less appeal for her, although to conform with the customs of their social circle she might occasionally make an appearance on the ski slopes in St Moritz – but never without her trademark jewelry.

Nonetheless, after nearly twelve years, the marriage began to disintegrate and ended in 1936 when Lydia sued her husband for divorce. Sir Henri then married his personal assistant and moved to Germany, his new wife's homeland. He obtained custody of Lilla and Olga, who experienced three years at the heart of Hitler's Third Reich before returning to England after the sudden death of their father in 1939. Lydia never remarried but spent the remainder of her life in Paris, living first in Neuilly-sur-Seine before moving to 88 Avenue Foch in the fashionable 16th arrondissement. Here she resumed her role as a talented hostess; her dinner parties were lavish and carefully planned, and were attended by both her closest friends and visiting dignitaries, particularly Americans.

Lydia did not just spend her time in Paris entertaining, however. In 1937, her benevolent efforts helping Russian emigrés were rewarded by Grand Duke Cyril of Russia, self-proclaimed head of the Romanovs following the death of his first cousin Tsar Nicholas II (although he was not recognized by the Dowager Empress Maria Feodorovna). The Duke granted Lydia the title 'Princess of the Don', the highest honour that could be conferred on a Russian who was not of royal blood. Furthermore, on two occasions she was awarded the Légion d'honneur: the first for her generosity in donating several important works of art to the Louvre, and the second for her assistance in the promotion of good diplomatic relations between France and the USA. It was perhaps this second award that she received with the greatest pride, for it acknowledged the social skills she valued so highly. Lydia remained in Paris until her death in 1980, and continued to enjoy her various social and philanthropic activities until the end. In the words of one of her daughters, she 'was always fun'.

In line with her contemporaries, Lydia constantly updated her jewelry and there were few pieces in her impressive collection that remained in their original form. Those that were unchanged included an Art

Sir Henri and Lady Deterding dressed for presentation at court in the late 1920s. She is wearing the emerald and diamond necklace set with the 'Polar Star'.

A pair of carved emerald, ruby and diamond 'Tutti Frutti' lapel clips by Cartier, Paris, late 1920s.

Page 36
A 1930s studio portrait of Lady
Deterding by Dorothy Wilding
and a 1930s flowerhead diamond
brooch by Boucheron.

A ruby and diamond bracelet
by Cartier, *c.* 1930s. It is set with
seventy-two cushion-shaped
rubies in four rows, with circular-
cut and baguette diamond
motifs.

Below
Lady Deterding giving her two
daughters, Lilla and Olga, a ride
on her skis, near her chalet in St
Moritz, January 1934.

Above
A 1930s sapphire and diamond bracelet by Cartier, London. The three step-cut sapphires, together weighing about 19 cts, are from the Kashmir mines, which have produced some of the most sought-after sapphires in the world.

Left
An archive photograph showing the two sapphire bracelets, which could be joined by a central motif and used as a necklace or bandeau. Lady Deterding had them altered a couple of times.

Opposite
A group of jewels created by Cartier in the late 1920s for Lady Deterding. From top left: an enamel and gem-set vanity case with watch, the black enamel lid set with a motif in diamonds, carved emeralds and rubies; a pair of sapphire and diamond pendent ear clips, the tops with circular-cut and baguette diamonds supporting a pair of cabochon sapphire drops; and an evening bag, the frame decorated with mottled blue and black enamel, and the clasp formed by a carved and pierced jade globe accented with diamonds.

A coral, onyx and diamond
pendent watch by Cartier, c. 1925
(above), and a platinum, coral
and diamond frame created by
Cartier to contain a photograph
of Lady Deterding (left).

Opposite
A stained chalcedony set
from Cartier, late 1930s.

Deco ruby and diamond bracelet by Cartier, set with four rows of cushion-shaped rubies and with diamond motifs (p. 39). She also kept one of Cartier's most sensational jewels: a pair of carved emerald, ruby and diamond 'Tutti Frutti' lapel clips. Each mitre-shaped clip was set with a large carved emerald leaf within borders of brilliant-cut and baguette diamonds and ruby beads (p. 38). Also by Cartier were some splendid Kashmir sapphires set in a bracelet (p. 40), some sapphire pendent earrings and several stylish gold and diamond compacts and cigarette cases to complete her outfits, as well as evening bags decorated with gemstones and colourful enamels (p. 41). It is evident that Cartier was her jeweler of choice.

During the late 1930s, chalcedony, stained a mauvish blue reminiscent of lavender jade, became extremely fashionable, as exemplified by the wonderful *parure* created for the Duchess of Windsor by the French designer Suzanne Belperron. Lydia had a stylish necklace of large coloured chalcedony beads, which were connected by a gold clasp set with pink tourmaline and emerald beads and supported gold pod motifs. To match the necklace Cartier made a pair of pendent earrings, further embellished with rubies and diamonds (p. 43).

The most important pieces Lydia possessed were three jewels of Russian provenance. In a studio portrait taken in the early 1930s by the society

photographer Dorothy Wilding, Lydia wears a superb pearl and diamond pendant. Made in the mid-19th century, it had an Imperial Russian provenance and was one of her most treasured possessions. In 1866, the Tsesarevich Alexander Alexandrovich (the future Alexander III), who had become heir to the throne on the death of his older brother a year earlier, married his deceased brother's fiancée, Princess Marie Sophie Frederikke Dagmar of Denmark. As an Imperial bride she became known as Maria Feodorovna and was the mother of the ill-fated Tsar Nicholas II. There are several images of her as a young woman wearing the pearl and diamond pendant. Following the Revolution, the now Dowager Empress escaped Russia with her eldest daughter, the Grand Duchess Xenia Alexandrovna, and the pendant remained in her collection until her death in Denmark in 1928. It then passed into the hands of the Grand Duchess who sold it to Lady Deterding with a personal letter confirming its illustrious provenance. Most of the other jewels from the private collection of Maria Feodorovna were sold by the Grand Duchess and her sister Olga to King George V and Queen Mary.

The pendant was the second Russian piece Lydia obtained from the Grand Duchess Xenia's family. In the mid-1920s she acquired the 'Polar Star' (p. 46) from the collection of Prince Felix Yusupov, the Grand Duchess Xenia's son-in-law. He was one of the wealthiest and most powerful men in Russia before the Revolution, but is better known now as the probable assassin of Rasputin. The antique cushion-shaped diamond came from the mines at Golconda near Hyderabad in India, which have produced some of the finest stones in the world, such as the Koh-i-nûr and the 'Hope' blue diamond. The 41.28 cts 'Polar Star' derives its name from the eight-pointed star cut on its pavilion. Originally the property of Joseph Bonaparte, the elder brother of Napoleon, it was obtained by Princess Tatiana Yusupov in the 1820s and eventually inherited by Prince Felix. When Felix fled Russia he managed to take with him some of the more important jewels from the famous family collection, which he sold to help support their life in exile in Paris. In 1924, he started discussions with Cartier, who wished to buy the famous stone.

Although it has been reported that Lydia did not acquire the 'Polar Star' until 1928, information

Above
A pearl and diamond pendant originally in the collection of Empress Maria Feodorovna of Russia.

Opposite
A studio portrait by Dorothy Wilding. Lady Deterding is wearing the pearl and diamond pendant bought from the Grand Duchess Xenia Alexandrovna.

Opposite (inset)
The young Maria Feodorovna wearing the pearl and diamond pendant.

Above right
The emerald and diamond *sautoir* created by Cartier in 1921 for Princess Anastasia of Greece. It was repurchased by Cartier after her death in 1923 and the pendant sold to Lady Deterding.

Right
The historic 41.28 cts 'Polar Star' diamond.

Left
Lydia, Lady Deterding at a reception at the British Embassy in Paris in 1938. She is wearing the 'Polar Star' necklace with the step-cut emerald and pear-shaped drops positioned as they had been in the original *sautoir*. Prince Dmitri of Russia, son of the Grand Duchess Xenia, is on the right.

Opposite
The emerald pendant with the 41.28 cts 'Polar Star' diamond, mounted as a necklace for Lady Deterding by Cartier, London, in 1926.

from the Cartier archives suggests that it had already been incorporated into a sensational necklace for her by March 1926. The diamond was set as a pendant, surmounted by a large step-cut emerald and supporting two superb pear-shaped emerald drops mounted as a *lavallière*. It was then hung from a chain of brilliant-cut diamonds, connected at intervals by larger step-cut stones (p. 47).

The emerald pendant had previously formed the tassel of a spectacular emerald and diamond *sautoir* created by Cartier for Princess Anastasia of Greece in 1921, using the stones from two of her other jewels (p. 46). The Princess had previously been married to the American tin magnate William Bateman Leeds.

The vast fortune she inherited from him when he died in 1908 enabled her to amass a fabulous collection of jewels. She had married Prince Christophe, the brother of King Constantine I of Greece, in 1920. After her death in 1923 the emerald and diamond *sautoir* was bought back by Cartier and the pendant sold to Lady Deterding to be integrated into the necklace with the 'Polar Star'. A photograph from 1938 shows her wearing the necklace, but on that occasion the three emeralds were hanging together and the 'Polar Star' was set above them (p. 46). Some years later she created a new setting for the 'Polar Star' – by the time of the Christie's sale in 1980 it had been mounted by Boucheron as a magnifcent ring.

Opposite
A three-row pearl necklace with a sapphire and diamond clasp photographed over a portrait of Lydia, Lady Deterding by Alejo Vidal-Quadras, 1969, in which she is wearing the necklace together with a pair of pearl and diamond pendent ear clips by Cartier (below right).

Above left
A pair of diamond pendent earrings from the late 1960s. On each earring, a pear-shaped diamond is suspended from a circular-cut and baguette diamond surmount. Together these diamonds weigh almost 17 cts.

The diamond necklace that had once held the 'Polar Star' was to provide the setting for the third sensational Russian gem bought by Lady Deterding after the Revolution: the famous 'Azra' pearl. This black drop-shaped pearl was part of the Imperial Crown Jewels until 1783, when Catherine the Great gave it to one of her favourites, Prince Potemkin. In 1826, he bequeathed it to his niece Princess Tatiana Yusupov, and it remained in that family for over a century. On 30 March 1935, Prince Felix took the 'Azra' pearl and a round black button pearl to Boucheron in Paris to be mounted as a pendant on a string of 110 perfectly matched pearls. The two black pearls were joined together with a diamond motif created using the stones from one of the Prince's other jewels, including two pear-shaped, old-cut diamonds, each weighing 3.08 cts. Together with the much-admired

'Pelegrina' pearl and a pair of pearl earrings that also belonged to the Yusupovs, the necklace was displayed at the 'Exhibition of Russian Art' held that summer in Belgrave Square in London, where it caught the eye of Lady Deterding (p. 48). In addition to its great beauty and impressive history, another factor that might have strengthened Lydia's determination to possess this and the other Imperial jewels was her acquaintance with the Yusupov family. She may have regarded these transactions as a mutually agreeable means of helping her fellow Russians in exile with their financial difficulties after the Revolution.

Lydia was unfortunate enough to lose the 'Azra' pearl 'somewhere in Paris', so Cartier dismantled the original pearl necklace and reset the remaining black pearl and diamond pendant in the diamond necklace that had once held the 'Polar Star' and emerald

A. Vidal-Quadras '64

Opposite
A ruby and diamond *parure* by
Cartier, Paris, 1951, comprising
a necklace, pendent earrings
and a bangle. The necklace is
set with five graduating palmette
motifs, with oval-shaped rubies
and baguette and brilliant-cut
diamonds, which could be
detached and worn as clips.
The pendants on the earrings
could also be detached.

Left
Lydia, Lady Deterding
photographed at a reception
in Paris in the 1970s wearing
her pearl, sapphire and diamond
necklace, together with a
diamond brooch by Cartier,
Paris. At the centre of the
brooch is a 47.12 cts step-cut
sapphire (below).

pendant from Princess Anastasia (p. 49). It was in this form that the necklace and pendant appeared at the 1980 sale of Lydia, Lady Deterding's jewelry.

Lydia would often visit Cartier to exchange pieces or to have them redesigned. Her stunning ruby and diamond *parure* came from Cartier in 1951 (p. 52); the following decade she bought a 47.00 cts sapphire and had it mounted at the centre of a striking diamond flowerhead brooch (above). Also from Cartier were a beautiful turquoise and diamond *parure*, comprised of a necklace, pendent earrings and a bracelet, and a very elegant canary yellow and white diamond rose brooch with matching ear clips that she bought in 1969. The collection as a whole, consisting of pieces with an important provenance as well as a very personal selection of the best of modern jewelry, revealed an owner confident of her own taste and with a high regard both for quality and beauty. These jewels perhaps give us the best insight into the mysterious Lydia, Lady Deterding. ✖

The Duchess of Windsor

3

It is difficult to compare the Duchess of Windsor's jewelry collection with any other. It not only consisted of jewels that had been chosen by a king to give to the woman he loved and gave up his throne for, but also included some of the finest designs by the great 20th-century jewelers, particularly from the 1930s and 1940s. 'The Jewels of the Duchess of Windsor' were offered for auction by Sotheby's, Geneva, in April 1987, a year after she died, and provided fresh insight into the life, tastes and style of the Windsors.

The story of the relationship between King Edward VIII and the already once-divorced American Wallis Warfield Simpson is one of the most romantic and controversial of all time. To the British public – as well as to those in the Empire – the Prince of Wales had been the epitome of a Prince Charming: handsome, fashionable, modernizing. He grew up surrounded by historic and important works of art, which instilled in him a taste for beautiful objects, and in particular jewelry – a passion inherited from his mother, Queen Mary. Many of the pieces he commissioned for Wallis were based on his own ideas, and he spent many pleasurable hours with the designers, offering his suggestions. It was then up to her to have a suitable dress designed to complement the jewel. The uniting of two such stylish people resulted in distinctive collections, not only of jewelry but also of furniture and works of art.

Bessie Wallis Warfield's date of birth is generally agreed to be 19 June 1896 (she did not have a birth certificate). Her father died of consumption just five months later, when he was only 26, and thereafter Wallis's mother had to rely heavily on help from her wealthy brother-in-law Solomon Warfield and her sister Bessie Merryman in raising and educating Wallis in Baltimore, Maryland. Aunt Bessie continued to give emotional support to Wallis throughout her life.

When Wallis first met the Prince of Wales in January 1931, she was already married for the second time. Her first marriage, to an American naval aviator, Earl Winfield Spencer, had ended in divorce in 1927; in July 1928 in London, she married Ernest Simpson, an Anglo-American businessman. She loved life in the capital with its glamorous social occasions, and became a popular hostess, admired for her sense of style and elegance. The Simpsons were soon mixing in circles with access to the Prince of Wales and by the end of 1931 Wallis had not only been presented at court but was also inviting the heir to the throne to dinner. The Prince was attracted by Wallis's direct manner and he was soon asking the couple – and increasingly Wallis alone – to his weekend retreat, Fort Belvedere, near Windsor. As he later wrote, this new relationship was 'destined to change the whole course of my life'.

By the summer of 1934, Wallis was the Prince's only favourite, and although the romance was becoming known about in high society, it obviously had to be kept secret from the wider world. The couple enjoyed sending each other coded messages, both in their correspondence and – most intriguingly – engraved on gifts of jewelry. The earliest dated inscription was on a necklet of twelve charms. A cushion-shaped plaque decorated with a red enamel number 3 was dated on the reverse: '9/4/34 march 12th 1934 14/5/34'. No one knows what the dates allude to, but the other charms on the necklet record weekends at Fort Belvedere, holidays together, often with Aunt Bessie and other friends, and events mentioned in letters and diaries. The necklet was a simple but highly personal piece, and when the original estimate of SF2,000–3,000 was exceeded at the 1987 sale by a final bid of SF198,000, it became obvious that buyers were willing to pay a high price for what they regarded as a piece of history.

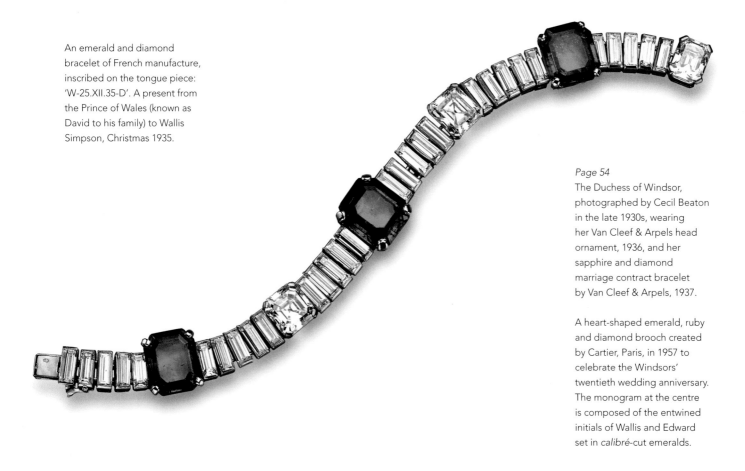

An emerald and diamond bracelet of French manufacture, inscribed on the tongue piece: 'W-25.XII.35-D'. A present from the Prince of Wales (known as David to his family) to Wallis Simpson, Christmas 1935.

Page 54
The Duchess of Windsor, photographed by Cecil Beaton in the late 1930s, wearing her Van Cleef & Arpels head ornament, 1936, and her sapphire and diamond marriage contract bracelet by Van Cleef & Arpels, 1937.

A heart-shaped emerald, ruby and diamond brooch created by Cartier, Paris, in 1957 to celebrate the Windsors' twentieth wedding anniversary. The monogram at the centre is composed of the entwined initials of Wallis and Edward set in *calibré*-cut emeralds.

The increasing intimacy between the couple can be gauged by the gold Latin cross pendant that Wallis gave to the Prince on 25 November 1934 and the similar platinum Latin cross pendant that he gave to her, which is inscribed and dated: 'WE are too 25-XI-34.' It was catalogued as 'a punning allusion to Mrs Simpson and the Prince of Wales' (WE) feelings for one another: WE (Wallis and Edward) are also in love, and WE two are in love.' The fact that the Prince's brother George, Duke of Kent, was to be married a few days later, on 29 November 1934, to Princess Marina of Greece might help to explain the inscription. The platinum Latin cross pendant was one of nine similar crosses, the others all gem-set, which were attached to a diamond bracelet made by Cartier in 1935 (p. 63).

When Edward was Prince of Wales, he was able to conduct his relationship with Mrs Simpson reasonably discreetly, although it caused increasing concern within court circles. In the press, Wallis was always referred to as 'a friend'. He showed his love by gifts of jewelry, including an impressive emerald and diamond bracelet (above), a Christmas gift in 1935, together with an elegant emerald and diamond necklace created

by Van Cleef & Arpels. The necklace was a double line of baguette diamonds, of alternating lengths, and step-cut Colombian emeralds (p. 57). He also gave her a pair of ear clips with a step-cut emerald in a border of baguette diamonds. Wallis gave him a gold cigarette case by Cartier, engraved with a map of Europe, with the routes of their holidays together shown in enamel and a gemstone set at the places they had visited. One of the trips was aboard Daisy Fellowes's yacht, the *Sister Anne*, which she had generously lent them. In fact, Christmas 1935 was a distressing time because of George V's declining health. On 20 January 1936, the King died and the Prince ascended the throne as Edward VIII. He was to reign for less than a year.

Against a background of increased political tension in Europe with the growing power of Nazi Germany and the outbreak of civil war in Spain, the British government, the King and his family became increasingly embroiled in the deepening relationship between the monarch and Mrs Simpson. Edward was finding it difficult to carry out his new royal duties without the presence of Wallis, who was still married to Ernest. For all of them it was a time of great uncertainty.

Wallis Simpson, photographed by Cecil Beaton in the grounds of the Château de Candé in 1937, prior to her marriage to the Duke of Windsor. She is wearing the famous lobster dress by Schiaparelli and the emerald and diamond Van Cleef & Arpels necklace ordered by the Duke in 1935 when he was Prince of Wales. The original design is shown at right.

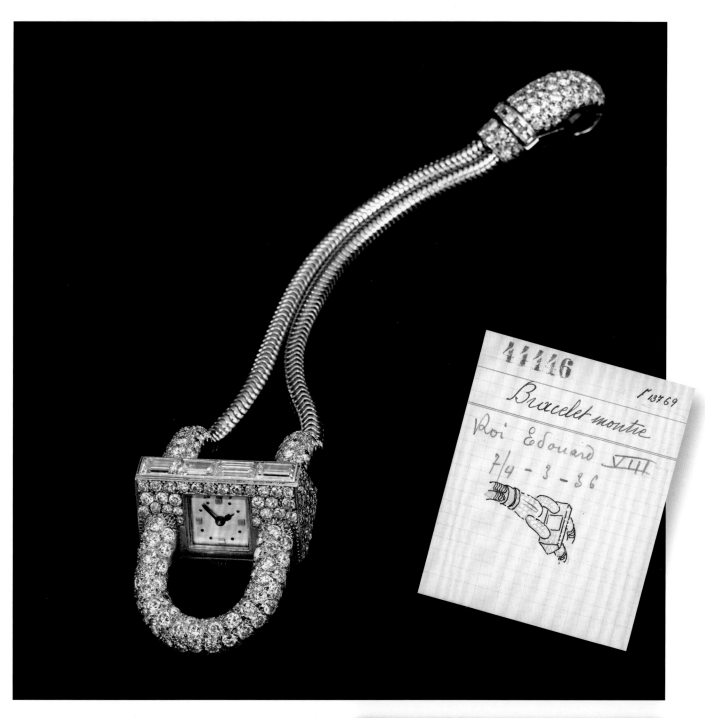

Opposite
A studio portrait of Wallis by Cecil Beaton, 1936. She is wearing ruby and diamond creole earclips by Van Cleef & Arpels.

A platinum and diamond 'Cadenas' bracelet watch with the original design drawing. The watch was a present from King Edward VIII to Wallis. The case is inscribed in a facsimile of the King's handwritting: 'For their 3 anniversary 12-III-36 and Our tub 17-III-36'.

Opposite above
Mrs Simpson wearing the full
ruby and diamond Van Cleef &
Arpels *parure* that she received
in 1936 from King Edward VIII.

Opposite below
Designs for the ear clips and
bracelet of the *parure* created by
Van Cleef & Arpels in 1936. The
bracelet was inscribed on the
clasp, 'Hold Tight 27-iii-36' – a
message of love and reassurance
when the relationship between
the King and Mrs Simpson was
causing increased concern in
court circles. Wallis later had
the ear clips redesigned.

Above
HRH The Prince of Wales,
photographed by Hugh Cecil
in 1935, wearing the uniform
of colonel-in-chief of the
Welsh Guards.

Left
The design of the ruby and
diamond necklace of the *parure*
Mrs Simpson is wearing in the
photograph opposite. Three
years later it was redesigned by
Van Cleef & Arpels (p. 93).

Edward reassured Wallis and indicated his love through his presents. One particularly clear message was inscribed on the clasp of a simple yet elegant bracelet made of Burmese rubies and diamonds by Van Cleef & Arpels, the creation of one of their best Paris designers, René Sim Lacaze: 'Hold Tight 27-iii-36' (pp. 60 and 93). A few days later, the King wrote to Wallis, in the infantile language they reserved for their private correspondence, that 'THEY say that THEY liked this bracelet and that THEY want you to wear it always in the evening.'

On an earlier gift from Wallis to Edward, in 1935, she had used the same phrase, 'Hold Tight', and on this diamond dress suite she had added the date of her birthday to the cufflinks. This had proved an excellent reminder, as on her fortieth birthday on 19 June 1936 she received from the King a splendid necklace of Burmese rubies and diamonds by Van Cleef & Arpels. The original version can be seen in contemporary photographs and in the designs in the firm's archives (pp. 60 and 61), but when the necklace came to auction it was in a completely different form (pp. 92 and 93). Wallis was a woman who not only kept up with fashion but virtually led it. The original design of the necklace had soon become outdated, and in 1939 René Sim Lacaze was commissioned to redesign the jewel. The transformation was stunning: the rubies and diamonds were mounted as an *entrelac de rubans* collar supporting a detachable tassel, with a few stones added. The result was a masterpiece of the jeweler's craft. Wallis wore it with a matching pair of earrings that had also been updated from their original 1936 design of loops of ruby and baguette diamonds by Van Cleef & Arpels. When they appeared in the 1987 auction they had been altered yet again. Cartier had remounted them as stylized flowerhead clusters in 1965.

In the spring of 1936 the King indicated to Ernest Simpson that he wished him to end his marriage to Wallis and by July divorce proceedings were set in motion. As Edward and Mrs Simpson cruised the Dalmatian coast on Lady Yule's yacht the *Nahlin* that summer, they discussed their future. Edward hoped they could marry before his coronation, scheduled for May 1937, naively little realizing the opposition there would be to the head of the Church of England marrying a twice-divorced woman. Photographs of the cruise appeared in the foreign press but not in British papers.

The sapphire and diamond marriage contract bracelet that Van Cleef & Arpels made for the Duke of Windsor as a wedding gift for his bride (top). It is inscribed inside: 'For our Contract 18-V-37'. The central motif is decorated with invisibly set cushion-shaped sapphires – the new setting that the French firm had patented the year before. The original design (above) was subsequently modified.

<table>
<tr><td>

Top
The Duke and Duchess of
Windsor, photographed by Cecil
Beaton after their marriage at
the Château de Candé, 3 June
1937. The Duchess is wearing the
sapphire and diamond bracelet.

</td><td>

Above
A diamond bracelet by Cartier
c. 1935, supporting nine gem-set
Latin crosses, all engraved and
dated. Left to right: in sapphire,
emerald, ruby and diamond: *Our
marriage Cross Wallis 3.VI.37*

</td><td>

David; in aquamarine, *God save
the King for Wallis 16.VII.36*;
in amethyst, *Appendectomy
Cross Wallis 31-VIII-44 David*;
in emerald, *X Ray Cross Wallis
– David 10.7.36*; in baguette
diamonds, *The Kings* (sic) *Cross*

</td><td>

God bless WE 1-3-36; in ruby,
*Wallis – David St Wolfgang 22-
9-3[5]*; in yellow sapphire,*"Get
Well" Cross Wallis Sept. 1944
David*; in sapphire, *Wallis – David
23-6-35*; in platinum, *WE are too*
(sic) *25-XI-34*.

</td></tr>
</table>

The renowned English artist Gerald Brockhurst, photographed in his studio in Chelsea, working on a portrait of the Duchess of Windsor. He is painting the Van Cleef & Arpels 'Hawaii' brooch (see the jeweler's design below). The portrait, completed in June 1939, had pride of place in the Windsors' home in the Bahamas, where the Duke was Governor during the Second World War.

Opposite
The Duke and Duchess of Windsor, photographed by Roger Schall at the Château de la Croë in Cap d'Antibes in the South of France, which they leased in 1938. The couple still hoped that they would be allowed to make England their permanent home. Wallis is wearing the yellow gold 'Hawaii' brooch by Van Cleef & Arpels, designed as a bouquet of flowers and set with rubies and 24 blue and yellow sapphires weighing over 100 cts.

A ruby and diamond bangle, given by the Duke of Windsor to the Duchess in 1938 as a wedding anniversary gift. It is inscribed on the inside: 'For our first anniversary of June third'. This jewel was created by Cartier using the ruby and diamond clusters from a 1937 necklace, shown at top in a photograph from the Cartier, Paris, archives. The two cushion-shaped Burmese rubies weigh 36.15 cts. Cartier remounted them as the terminals for the bangle.

The divorce petition was heard on 27 October, the date the couple thereafter regarded as that of their engagement. To mark the occasion, the King gave his future bride a ring with an exceptionally fine Colombian emerald of 19.77 cts bought from Cartier (p. 90). It was mounted in a plain platinum shank with two baguette diamond shoulders and the ring was inscribed: 'WE are ours now 27 x 36', a simple but bold statement. According to an entry in Marie Belloc Lowndes's diary, the emerald had been acquired by Cartier in Baghdad,

Opposite above and below
The Duke and Duchess of Windsor at the Ritz Hotel in Madrid, having fled France in June 1940 after the German invasion. She is wearing the flamingo brooch created by Jeanne Toussaint at Cartier, Paris, 1940. The stones were reused from other pieces owned by the Duchess.

but was originally double the size. Cartier decided that the market for such a gem was limited and had it cut into two stones. One was bought by an American millionaire and the other by the King. It is more likely, however, that this stone came from the emerald and diamond *sautoir* once owned by Princess Anastasia of Greece, the former Nancy Leeds. Some of those emeralds had come from the Sultan of Turkey and were bought back by Cartier, who had made the *sautoir*, after the death of the princess in 1923. The largest emeralds were remounted in a necklace for the Maharaja of Nawanagar and it is possible that much later Cartier sold one of the remaining magnificent emeralds to Edward. Whatever its origins, the stone is superb. To keep abreast of changing fashions, it was remounted in 1958 in a diamond setting by Cartier, Paris, but Wallis kept the original mount with its inscription.

At the beginning of December, the British public finally became aware of the King's liaison with Mrs Simpson and matters reached a crisis point. Wallis secretly left England to stay with friends in France while Edward held meetings with his advisers and government officials to find a way forward. Morganatic

The original design of the diamond head ornament the Duchess is wearing in the photograph opposite. The two lateral wing elements could be detached and worn as clips.

Opposite
The Duchess of Windsor, photographed by Cecil Beaton, wearing an array of jewels from her collection, including the diamond head ornament, 1936, and the emerald, diamond and ruby brooch, 1937, by Van Cleef & Arpels.

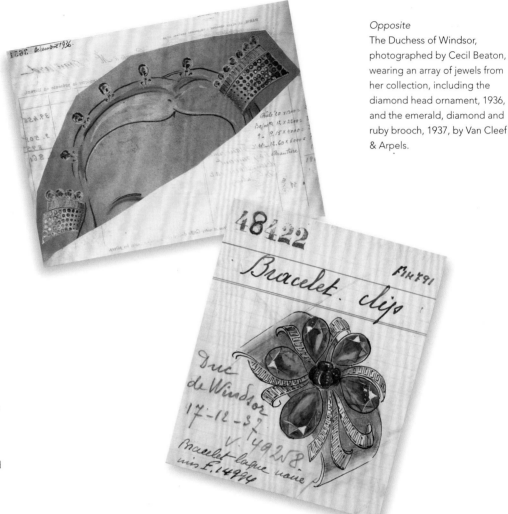

The design of the Van Cleef & Arpels brooch seen in the photograph opposite. It was set with five pear-shaped emeralds recorded as weighing 14.63, 7.85, 6.72, 6.66 and 5.85 cts, baguette diamonds and cabochon rubies. The brooch could also be mounted on a bangle of black enamel. In 1960, this brooch, together with the Duchess's double diamond leaf necklace, were used by Cartier to create an emerald and diamond necklace (p. 91).

marriage was ruled out and finally, refusing to renounce Wallis, he gave up his throne instead. On 10 December 1936, the King signed the Instrument of Abdication in the presence of his three brothers at Fort Belvedere and swore allegiance to his successor, his brother Bertie, now styled King George VI. Edward, with the new title of Duke of Windsor, delivered his abdication speech to the nation by radio and left the country the same evening. He would never live in England again.

The sensitivity of the situation and the divorce laws of the time necessitated an enforced separation period (the divorce was not finalized until May and might have been jeopardized if the couple had met). Edward headed for Austria, where he was the guest of Baron Eugène de Rothschild and his American wife, Kitty, at Schloss Enzesfeld. Once again, the couple had to spend Christmas apart, and Edward sent Wallis

another jewel by Lacaze in the form of a ruby and diamond clip designed as two *feuilles de houx* (holly leaves). The original clip fitting of this brooch was retained by Wallis for sentimental reasons. It was inscribed 'No more like this Christmas 1936 Make come quickly'. The stones in this brooch were invisibly set, then a new technique but one for which Van Cleef & Arpels are now famous. This is one of the best-known examples: the stones are held by small grooves on their pavilions and as all this work is at the back of the jewel no metal can be seen from the front (p. 93).

There were several other sentimental gifts during these months the couple had to spend apart, culminating in the magnificent sapphire and diamond *jarretière* bracelet by Van Cleef & Arpels, which Lacaze designed to celebrate the finalizing of the couple's marriage contract according to French law on 18 May 1937.

The Duchess of Windsor photographed by Horst in the late 1940s, wearing a gown by Mainbocher that provides a canvas for her colourful gem-set bib necklace by Cartier, Paris (opposite).

Below
A photograph from the Cartier archives, Paris, of a ruby bead necklace created for the Duchess in 1949. This necklace was inspired by Indian designs in which the clasps were made from silk thread. Cartier created the jewel using gold chains instead, replacing the usual silk tassels with two terminals of gold-mounted cabochon emeralds, ruby beads and diamonds. In 1963, Cartier created a brooch from the jewel, remounting the clasp and the two 'Hindou' tassel drops. The chains that connected the drops were later shortened.

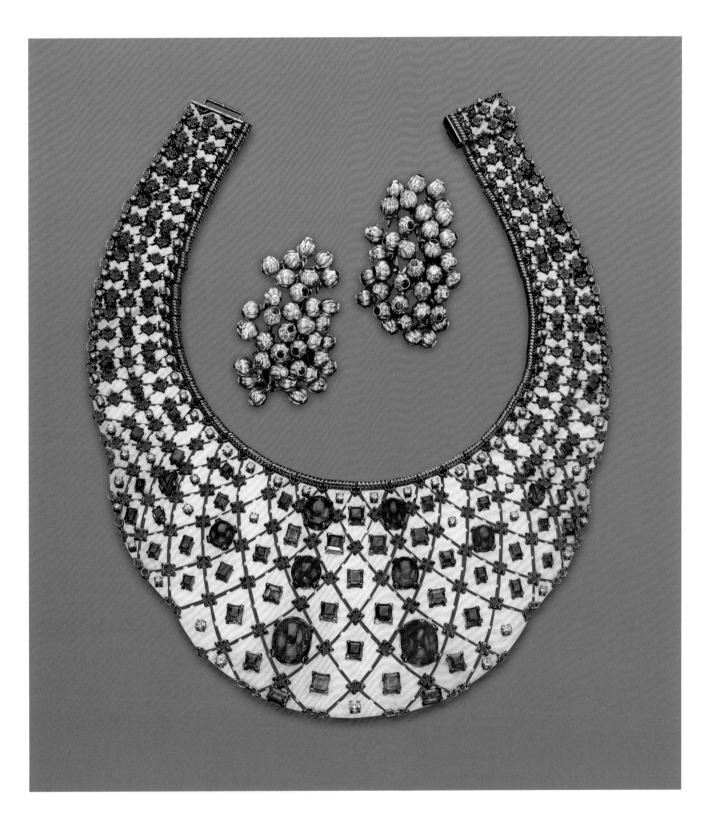

A gem-set bib necklace created for the Duchess by Cartier, Paris, in 1945. It is composed of lozenge-shaped motifs in yellow gold in an articulated design set with cabochon and step-cut rubies and emeralds, and brilliant-cut diamonds. As was the case with other jewels, the Duchess supplied Cartier with pieces she no longer wanted so that the stones could be reused. In this instance, two brooches, two pairs of earrings and a ring.

Centre
A pair of Cartier gold and gem-set ear clips designed as a cascade of articulated fluted gold beads set with rubies, emeralds and circular-cut diamonds.

The bracelet was designed as a band of baguette and circular-cut diamonds, with a large central clasp in a stylized bow shape invisibly set with cushion-shaped sapphires that concealed the inscription, 'For our Contract 18-v-37' (p. 62).

The wedding took place on 3 June 1937 at the Château de Candé in France. In the wedding portraits taken by Cecil Beaton, Wallis, now Duchess of Windsor (although notably not granted the status of Her Royal Highness), is wearing her Cartier Latin Cross bracelet from 1935. Each cross had an inscription relating to some event of importance to the couple (p. 63). She treasured this bracelet all her life together with one made in the 1950s that had a series of charms set in diamonds in the shape of hearts of varying sizes, mostly made by Van Cleef & Arpels (p. 72). One charm, signed by Cartier, is a diamond heart that opens, revealing the words 'The heart has its reasons' (a quote from Pascal and later the title of the Duchess's autobiography) and, on the reverse, 'WE March 1951'. The Van Cleef & Arpels archives have a design for another charm bracelet made for Wallis that reproduced all the elements needed to create a Sidecar cocktail.

Following the marriage, the couple lived in France, although they hoped the exile would not be permanent. On their first wedding anniversary, the Duke gave his bride a spectacular ruby and diamond hinged penannular bangle by Cartier, Paris, inscribed, 'For our first anniversary of June third' (p. 66). The two large terminals were set with cushion-shaped Burmese rubies, together weighing 36.15 cts, in raised collets which were *pavé*-set all over with brilliant-cut diamonds. These terminals had originally been set as the centre of a necklace forming a crossover clasp. The same concept was used in a double-leaf necklace worn by the Duchess on many occasions (p. 87), often with the ruby bangle. Twenty years later, the Duke asked Cartier to make a heart-shaped brooch applied with the initials WE to mark another wedding anniversary (p. 54).

Somewhat surprisingly, even into the early days of the war the Windsors were commissioning remarkable examples of contemporary jewelry design. In 1940, Jeanne Toussaint at Cartier, Paris, created a flamingo clip using stones that had been unmounted from other pieces in the Duchess's collection (p. 67). After the conflict, during which the Duke was Governor of the Bahamas, Madame Toussaint designed a splendid bird of paradise brooch with a body formed by a cabochon sapphire of over 60 cts and a long articulated tail set with diamonds, emeralds and sapphires, again using unmounted jewels belonging to the couple. Unfortunately, this piece was stolen shortly after the couple acquired it in 1946 when they were staying with the Earl and Countess of Dudley at Ednam Lodge in Berkshire during a private visit to England. There has always been a certain amount of debate as to the extent of the Duchess's loss, but from all accounts it was small, for the bulk of her collection had remained in France, where the couple had finally settled.

Throughout their married life, the Windsors continued to acquire extremely interesting jewels. The Duchess became famous for her decorative bib necklaces. One was designed by Cartier, Paris, in October 1945, and was composed of a series of lozenge-shaped motifs in yellow gold, in a draped articulated design, each one set with cabochon and step-cut rubies and emeralds and brilliant-cut diamonds (p. 71). To realize this unique piece, two gem-set brooches, two pairs of earrings and a ring were dismantled, and the stones were also used for a pair of ear clips set with articulated fluted gold beads, each one inset with a diamond, an emerald or a ruby. Perhaps the most stunning of these bib necklaces was the one created in 1947 by Cartier, Paris (p. 74). The lattice design was set with step-cut amethysts, brilliant-cut diamonds and turquoises, on a chain of Prince of Wales linking. Cartier also made a pair of ear clips, a brooch and a bracelet to go with the necklace. The combination of hues created a fashion that many ladies of the period picked up on.

In 1949, Cartier created an unusual necklace of Indian inspiration, with two rows of ruby beads (p. 70).

The Duchess of Windsor, photographed by Dorothy Wilding in 1955, wearing the charm bracelet set with rubies and diamonds, c. 1950, illustrated. The charms are by Van Cleef & Arpels and Cartier. The Duchess is wearing on her left hand the 'McLean' cushion-shaped diamond weighing 31.26 cts, the Cartier ear clips (p. 71) and her pearl and diamond pendant (p. 94). Below the photograph is the 47.14 cts fancy intense yellow diamond that the Duke bought for the Duchess in 1951 from Harry Winston to complement her other yellow diamonds and set in a ring. The stone was later acquired by Estée Lauder, set in a pendant and sold by the Lauder family in 2012 in aid of the Breast Cancer Research Foundation. It is now known as 'The Windsor Heart'.

A bib necklace and matching ear clips created by Cartier, Paris, in 1947 for Wallis, set with step-cut amethysts weighing over 158 cts, supplied by the Duke, and turquoises, brilliant-cut and baguette diamonds in a twisted gold lattice design suspended from a chain of Prince of Wales linking.

Opposite
The Duke and Duchess of Windsor at the ball held in aid of cancer research in the orangerie of the Palace of Versailles, June 1953. She is wearing the amethyst and turquoise bib necklace with matching ear clips.

The Duke and Duchess of Windsor in a photograph by Philippe Halsman that was used for the cover of *Life* magazine in May 1950. She is wearing a gold rope chain from which two engraved gold caps with articulated gold balls are suspended (left).

Opposite
The Windsors in the 1950s, photographed by Arthur Rothstein. She is wearing the amethyst, turquoise and diamond brooch, with a terminal of conical form set with an oval amethyst of 30.30 cts, created by Cartier, Paris, in 1950 (below).

76

The Duke and Duchess of Windsor with the former Senator from Maryland, Millard Tydings, and Mrs B. H. Griswold at the Crusade Ball in aid of the American Cancer Society, Baltimore, Maryland, 14 January 1955. The Duchess is wearing a simple gown that provides a backdrop for her jewels, in a style that showed off her jewelry and became her trademark. Pinned to her dress are two yellow diamond clips by Harry Winston, purchased in 1948, each set with a pear-shaped diamond weighing 52.13 and 40.81 cts respectively (far left). She is also wearing the yellow diamond pendent earrings set with two brilliant-cut diamonds of 5.17 and 5.18 cts and two pear-shaped diamonds weighing 8.13 and 8.01 cts, acquired by Winston to accompany the clips. In 1968, the Duchess had the pendent earrings reset by Cartier as ear clips in a yellow diamond *pavé*-set mount, as illustrated at left. Around the Duchess's neck is a necklace from 1950 by Tony Duquette in two-coloured gold, *mabé* pearls, tourmaline and quartz, designed as an articulated garland of leaves and flowers. She also wears a cultured pearl cuff bangle with a matching ring by Suzanne Belperron, from *c.* 1940 (opposite).

Above and right
A gold and diamond *nécessaire du soir* by Cartier, Paris, 1947. The interior is inscribed and dated, 'Wallis from Edward 1947'. It may have been a tenth wedding anniversary present.

Left
An evening bag, *c.* 1930. The frame is *pavé*-set throughout with circular-cut diamonds, diamond-tipped ruby beads and black enamel motifs.

A gold and diamond *nécessaire du soir* by Cartier, Paris, 1947, designed as an egg with rope-work borders, engraved on one side with the royal arms as borne by the Duke of Windsor, on the other with the entwined letters WW (for Wallis Windsor) beneath a coronet. The ring is set with brilliant-cut diamonds and the thumb piece with a rose diamond.

The gold clasp was encrusted with diamonds, emeralds and rubies. The two long gold chains that hung over the Duchess's shoulders supported two large spheres set with cabochon emeralds and ruby beads. When this jewel was altered by Cartier in 1963, the clasp and the spheres became an elegant brooch and the ruby beads were fashioned into dramatic creole earrings. The brooch did not appear in the 1987 auction, but six years later it was sold in New York as the property of 'a member of a European Royal House'.

In the postwar years, the American jeweler Harry Winston played an important role in adding some fine gemstones to the Windsors' collection. In 1948 he sold them a superb pair of fancy yellow diamonds, which he intimated had formerly belonged to royalty fallen on hard times. The well-matched pear-shaped stones weighed 40.81 and 52.13 cts and were mounted as lapel clips (p. 79). In the correspondence between Winston and the Duchess about these diamonds, she wrote that she could not think of anything she would rather have than those two diamonds and then promptly asked him to supply her with earrings to match. He found two yellow diamonds of the same hue, brilliant-cut of 5.17 and 5.18 cts. From each stone hung a pear-shaped fancy yellow diamond of, respectively, 8.13 and 8.01 cts. In 1968 these were remounted by Cartier, Paris, as ear clips with the placing of the stones reversed. The new mounts were *pavé*-set with yellow diamonds.

The Duke decided to complete the *parure* with a ring, and again it was Harry Winston who found a matching stone, which the Duke acquired on 9 April 1951. It was a heart-shaped, fancy yellow diamond of over 47 cts (p. 72). The stone was mounted in yellow gold, in an identical setting to the lapel clips. The Duchess treasured this ring, and there are photographs of her wearing it both alone and with the rest of the parure. This jewel did not appear in the 1987 sale and no one knew its whereabouts. It transpired that her friend Estée Lauder had bought it in the 1970s to help fund the Duchess's upkeep following the Duke's death in 1972. It was sold at Sotheby's, New York, in 2012 in aid of the Breast Cancer Research Foundation.

The Duchess of Windsor at a reception held at the Waldorf Astoria, New York, on 10 February 1959 in honour of the Mayor of West Berlin, Willy Brandt. She stands between Mrs Susan Wagner, wife of the Mayor of New York, and Mrs Rut Brandt. The Duchess is wearing the pear-shaped cabochon emerald and foiled diamond necklace (opposite) as a two-row choker, together with her gold, emerald-bead and rose diamond ear clips by Cartier, 1957. She is holding her gold and diamond *nécessaire du soir* by Cartier, 1947.

Opposite

An emerald and table-cut foiled diamond necklace, which was sold to the Windsors by Harry Winston in 1956. This exotic Indian necklace could be worn in three ways: one single row (as illustrated here); divided and worn as a two-row choker (above); or as a bib necklace, with the two rows connected at the back by two chains of gold Prince of Wales linking. In 1957, the Duchess had a pair of gold, emerald-bead and rose diamond earrings of Indian inspiration mounted by Cartier to wear with the necklace.

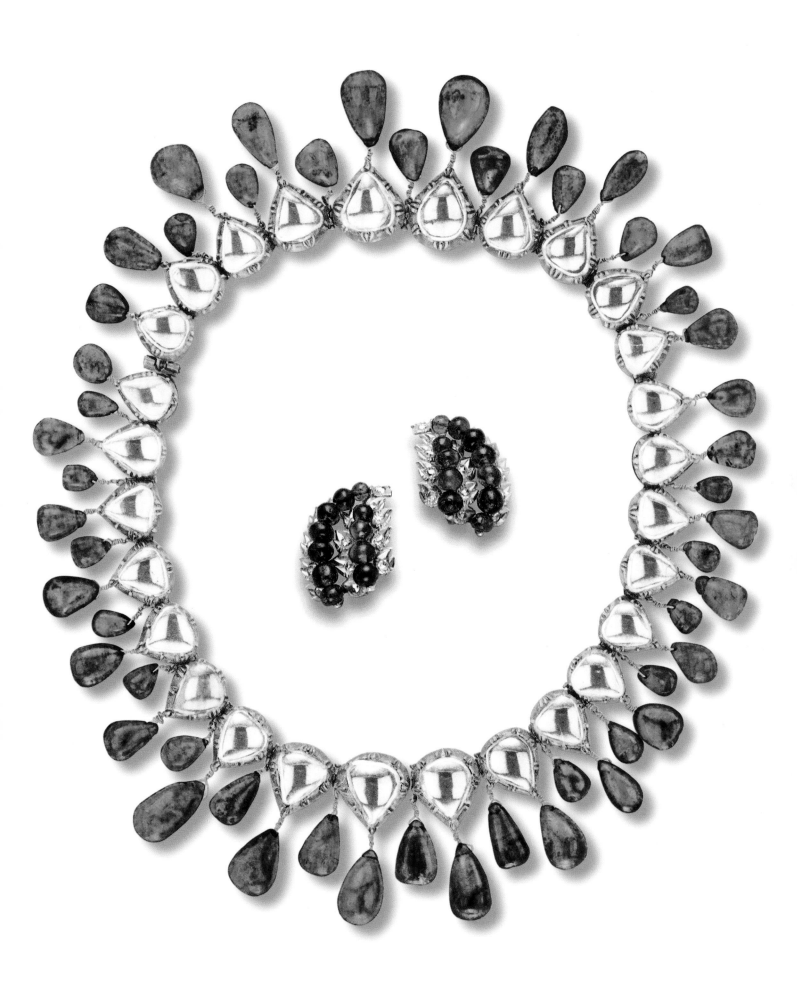

The Duke and Duchess of Windsor photographed by Cecil Beaton in the garden of their residence in the Bois de Boulogne in Paris, where the couple lived from the early 1950s. The Duchess is wearing the Cartier panther clip of 1948 and a pair of gold and emerald bangles, c. 1940 (see opposite).

By then 'The Windsor Heart' was set in a cluster of colourless, brilliant-cut diamonds as a pendant of a stylish Van Cleef & Arpels diamond necklace.

In 1960, the Duchess had the yellow diamonds certified for insurance purposes by De Beers in London. The stones were submitted to an exhaustive examination and were given a completely 'clean' certificate, which meant there was no possible doubt as to their quality. De Beers added that it was impossible for them to put a value on the stones as they were 'almost irreplaceable' and only Harry Winston could say what they were worth.

Among the Duchess's jewelry collection was a menagerie of animals, including an array of 'Great Cat' jewels that were the inspiration of Jeanne Toussaint, who developed a close relationship with the couple. She was nicknamed 'The Panther' by her companion Louis Cartier because of her passion for those animals,

whose skins adorned the floors of her apartment. As director of fine jewelry at Cartier from the 1930s, she worked with the designer Peter Lemarchand and together they created the 'Great Cat' jewels that were popular with fashionable women in the postwar years.

The Windsors began their collection with a panther clip in 1948, their first commission from Cartier after the Ednam Lodge theft. A gold panther decorated with black enamel spots and crouched on a large cabochon emerald weighing about 90 cts, it was Cartier's first fully three-dimensional cat jewel. They also bought a pair of ear clips to match the brooch (p. 85).

For nearly two decades the Windsors continued to purchase these magnificent cats (pp. 86–87). In 1949, they acquired a sapphire and diamond clip designed as a panther seated on a large cabochon sapphire of 152.35 cts, and in 1952 an onyx and diamond panther bracelet, though the matching clip was not bought until 1966.

As with many of these jewels, not only was the cat's body completely flexible but its neck was mounted in such a fashion that the angle of the head could be altered at whim. An onyx and fancy yellow diamond tiger bracelet was acquired in 1956 and the matching clip in 1959. Her cat acquisition in 1954 was somewhat more unusual: a lorgnette whose handle was in the shape of a tiger with a raised paw, made of gold and black enamel. In every case the design and workmanship were exquisite, giving these exotic cats power and beauty along with a strong feeling of movement.

As well as Toussaint, the Windsors patronized other well-known designers of the period, such as Suzanne Belperron, Fulco di Verdura, Seaman Schepps and David Webb. The latter created for the Duchess his own version of the 'jungle' jewels. These came in the form of delightful gem-set frogs decorated with enamel and set with diamonds and cabochon rubies. He also cleverly mounted the shells of Cuban tree snails (which the Duchess had collected on her travels) as ear clips – as did the French jewelers Darde et Fils.

In 1953, Harry Winston acquired from the Maharajah of Baroda a pair of cabochon emerald and table-cut foiled diamond anklets from which he created a stunning necklace (p. 83). He sold it to the Windsors in 1956 but with unfortunate consequences. A year later the Duchess wore the necklace to a ball in Paris that was also attended by the Maharani of Baroda. The piece caused a stir and when the Maharani was asked her opinion she agreed about its beauty but added, 'those emeralds used to be my anklets'. This did not amuse the Duchess, although she continued to wear the necklace (p. 82). In 1960, however, she exchanged it for another jewel with the proviso that Harry Winston would not sell the necklace to anyone who might have known about her ownership of it.

The jewel that she now owned was a very fine 48.95 cts pear-shaped emerald, which had once belonged to King Alfonso XIII of Spain, mounted with diamonds as a pendant. At the same time, the Duchess supplied Cartier with various jewels that could be unmounted, including a diamond brooch set with five pear-shaped emeralds that had been created by Van Cleef & Arpels in 1937 (pp. 68 and 69). These jewels were remounted as a necklace from which the newly acquired emerald pendant could be hung. The five emeralds, repolished, became the central motif of the stylish necklace (p. 91).

Top
A panther clip by Cartier, Paris, 1948. The gold panther, decorated with black enamel spots and pear-shaped emerald eyes, is seated on a cabochon emerald weighing approximately 90 cts. This was the first truly three-dimensional 'Great Cat' jewel created by Cartier, and the first panther jewel acquired by the Windsors.

Above
Ear clips by Cartier that match the panther brooch.

Below
A pair of gold bangles, each one set with a line of emerald beads, created by Suzanne Belperron, c. 1940.

The Duke and Duchess of Windsor dancing at the gala opening of the Lido cabaret in Paris on 10 December 1959. She is wearing her tiger articulated bracelet of 1956 as well as the diamond double-leaf necklace ordered by the Duke from Cartier, Paris, in 1937. The diamonds were reused in 1960 for her Cartier emerald necklace (p. 91). The Harry Winston diamond ear clips were remounted by Cartier in 1962.

Below left
A gold brooch of Italian manufacture, *c.* 1960, designed as a panther, the muzzle *pavé*-set with eight-cut diamonds, the body decorated with black enamel spots and the nose, eyes and ears in red enamel.

Below right
A lorgnette created by Cartier, Paris, in 1954, designed as a tiger in gold and black *champlevé* enamel, with pear-shaped emerald eyes. It was contained in a brocade pochette inscribed, 'Please return to HRH The Duchess of Windsor Reward.' Note the use of HRH.

Opposite
The magnificent 'Great Cat' jewels inspired by Jeanne Toussaint and acquired by the Duchess from Cartier between 1949 and 1966.

The Duchess of Windsor with
Princess Margrethe, Princess
René de Bourbon Parme, at
the Ritz Hotel in Paris for the
wedding of Princess Françoise
de Bourbon Parme and Prince
Eduoard de Lobkowicz in January
1960. The Duchess is wearing the
sapphire and diamond brooch
by Cartier (opposite, above) and
the cabochon sapphire drops in
their original 1947 Harry Winston
setting with the stones standing
erect (see below).

Opposite above and centre
A sapphire and diamond brooch
and ring created by Cartier, Paris,
in 1949, with the sapphires in
lighter and darker shades of blue.
The circular central sapphire in
the ring weighs 46.60 cts.

Opposite below
A sapphire and diamond
pendant by Cartier, Paris, 1951.
The cushion-shaped sapphire,
weighing 206.82 cts, is claw-set
within a border of brilliant-
cut and baguette diamonds.
The loop, set with two rows of
baguette diamonds, could be
detached and the pendant worn
as a brooch.

Right
A pair of diamond and sapphire
pendent ear clips, each with
a drop-shaped Burmese
cabochon sapphire suspended
from a diamond-set surmount
of stylized Prince of Wales'
feathers. The sapphires,
originally weighing together
75.51 cts, were purchased from
Harry Winston on 16 April 1947,
mounted as ear clips. The
sapphires were probably
reset by Cartier and weighed
75.33 cts after repolishing.

The Duchess loved to wear the necklace with her emerald ear clips, which had been remounted by Cartier at the same time as the necklace was created (p. 90).

The jewels that the Duke showered on his wife were all extremely fine examples of the work of contemporary designers. The only piece that the Duke is known to have received from his family is a single row necklace of twenty-eight natural pearls given to him by his mother, Queen Mary (p. 94). It is possible that this necklace is the same pearl necklace that King George V bought in May 1929 from the jewels of the Dowager Empress Maria Feodorovna of Russia, his aunt, who had died in exile in Denmark the year before. At that point, the necklace was strung with thirty-two pearls; it is probable that the Duchess had it shortened when Cartier created the diamond and platinum clasp in the 1950s. The quality and size of this extraordinary necklace are evidence of its imperial provenance. In some ways, Queen Mary gave her son an extremely important piece of jewelry but crucially one that was not strictly connected to the British monarchy.

The Duchess often chose to wear the pearl necklace with a large pearl and diamond pendant (p. 72). In a letter addressed to the Duchess of Windsor from Olga Tritt Precious Jewels in Madison Avenue, New York, dated 3 March 1948, Harold P. Davidson noted the interest she had 'expressed in our large pearl and we are most anxious to make every possible concession in order that you may have it. We will make a special export price of $5,000 for the pearl and in addition will make a diamond and platinum connection … so that it may be correctly hung from a pearl necklace.'

An advertisement for Olga Tritt, dated January 1929, publicized the fact that she dealt in antique Russian jewelry and pearls, so it is possible this pearl originated in a Russian princely collection. It was remounted in its present form by Cartier (p. 94). Among the Duchess's other pearl jewels was an attractive pair of pearl and diamond earrings made by Van Cleef & Arpels in 1957 and bought by the couple the next year (p. 94). They were set with a large black and a large white pearl, each within a border of diamonds. In 1964, the Duchess had an 18-mm pearl remounted as a ring by Cartier in a gold and diamond border of *entrelac de rubans* design on a reeded yellow gold shank (p. 94).

The 'McLean' diamond (p. 93) was probably Harry Winston's star contribution to the couple's collection.

The Duke and Duchess of Windsor at the Gallery of Modern Art, New York, for the opening of 'The Memorable Eisenhower Years' exhibition, 16 May 1967. She is wearing her emerald and diamond jewels, including the emerald and diamond ear clips remounted by Cartier in 1960 in a spiral border of marquise-shaped diamonds (illustrated left). The ear clips were originally set with baguette diamonds.

The emerald and diamond ring. The step-cut emerald, weighing 19.77 cts, was originally set in a platinum ring with baguette diamond shoulders by Cartier, London, 1936. Wallis kept the original mount, which was inscribed: 'WE are ours now 27 X 36'. The King and Mrs Simpson regarded that date as their engagement day since it was when she obtained her divorce decree. In 1958, Cartier, Paris, remounted the stone within the stylized leaf border with brilliant-cut diamonds shown here.

The emerald and diamond necklace, created by Cartier, Paris, in 1960, using the five emeralds from the Duchess of Windsor's brooch (design illustrated on p. 68) now repolished down to weights of 14.61, 7.82, 6.67, 6.61 and 5.82 cts, and the emerald and diamond pendant created in the same year by Harry Winston. This pendant is set with a 48.95 cts emerald that had once belonged to King Alfonso XIII of Spain. Cartier provided a clip fitting so that it could also be used as a brooch.

Above
The Duke and Duchess of Windsor with the hostess, Hélène Rochas, photographed by Raymond Depardon at the My Fair Lady Ball in Paris, 1965. The Duchess is wearing her ruby and diamond jewels, including her Van Cleef & Arpels invisibly set brooch mounted as a head ornament on her white egret feather. She is holding her Cartier *nécessaire du soir* from 1947.

Opposite (from the top)
The ruby and diamond necklace. This is the *entrelac de rubans* design created by Van Cleef & Arpels in 1939 using the rubies from the Duchess's 1936 necklace (pp. 60 and 61). The original inscription was kept on the clasp: 'My Wallis from her David 19.VI.36'. The tassel could also be worn as a brooch.

The cushion-shaped 'McLean' diamond, weighing 31.26 cts.

The ruby and diamond bracelet by Van Cleef & Arpels, Paris, 1936, inscribed on the clasp: 'Hold Tight 27-iii-36'. (See the original design on p. 60.)

The clip of the invisibly set ruby and diamond *feuilles de houx* brooch of 1936 was changed so that it could also be used as a head ornament. Wallis kept the original one, inscribed 'No more like this Christmas 1936 Make come quickly'. Christmas 1936 was a period of enforced separation for the couple.

A pair of invisibly set ruby and diamond ear clips by Van Cleef & Arpels, New York, in an ivy-leaf design.

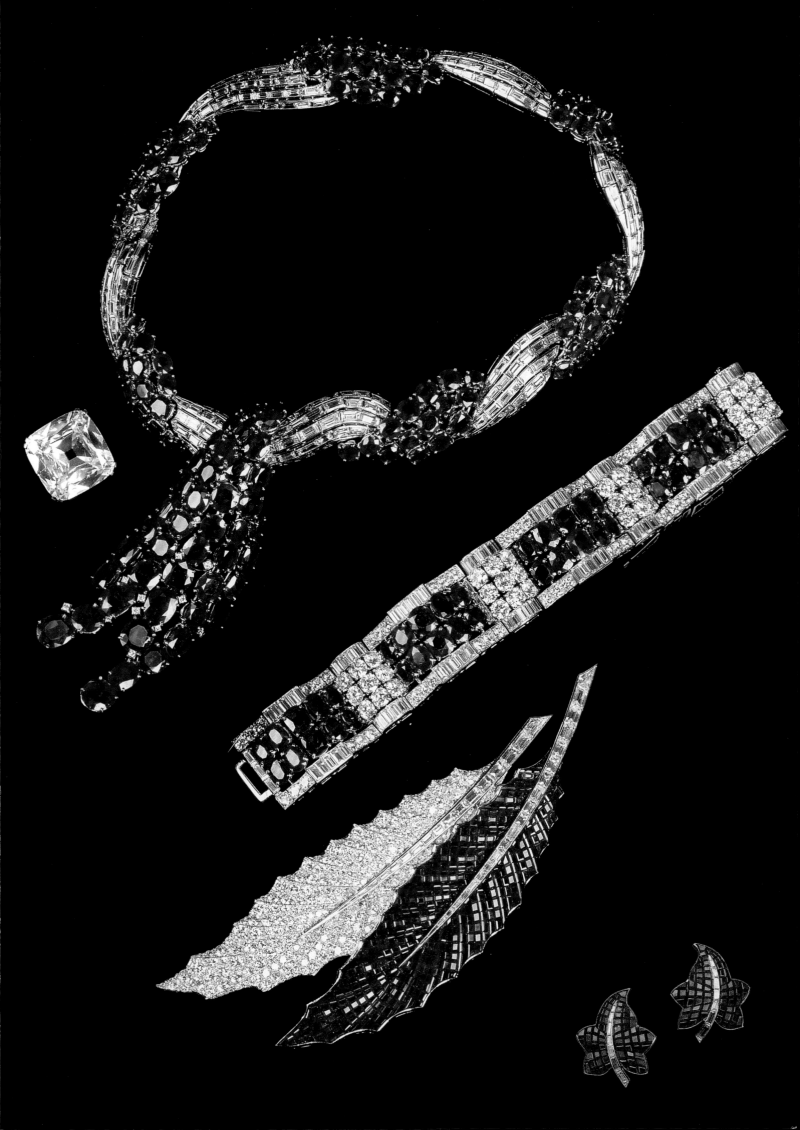

Opposite
The external string of 29 cultured pearls, created by Van Cleef & Arpels, 1964, holds a diamond and natural pearl pendant by Cartier, Paris, 1950. The inner necklace was strung by Cartier with 28 natural pearls that Queen Mary gave to the Duke of Windsor. The clasp is set in variously cut diamonds. In the centre is a ring set with a natural pearl measuring 18 mm in diameter, mounted by Cartier, Paris, in 1964 in a gold and brilliant-cut diamond border of

entrelac de rubans design on a reeded yellow gold shank. The pearl was originally set by Cartier in platinum, with two baguette diamond shoulders. The Duchess kept the setting and had the pearl replaced with an imitation black pearl. The ear clips by Van Cleef & Arpels, New York, 1957, have two natural button pearls, one black, measuring 18.2 mm, the other white, measuring 18.1 mm, each set in a border of pear-shaped and circular-cut diamonds.

Top right
The Prince of Wales diamond brooch, *c.* 1935.

Right
The Duchess of Windsor wearing the Prince of Wales brooch on her egret feather at the Baron Alexis de Redé's Bal des Têtes in 1957. She is with the Duke of Windsor, Princesse Ghislaine de Polignac and the couturier Elsa Schiaparelli. The Duchess also wears her Cartier double-leaf diamond necklace and Harry Winston diamond ear clips.

It was a cushion-shaped stone weighing 31.26 cts and of the finest D colour from the Golconda mines in India. Its former owner was Evelyn Walsh McLean, the celebrated Washington hostess and jewelry collector, known as the owner of the 'Hope' diamond, who died in 1947. Winston bought her collection in 1949 and in May 1950 sold the 'McLean' diamond to the Windsors mounted with two tapered baguette diamonds of 1.48 cts in a platinum setting.

The Windsor jewels fetched £31 million at the 1987 auction. The auctioneer, Nicholas Rayner, said at the time: 'The three elements of history, quality and design make the collection altogether unique.' It is perhaps unsurprising, therefore, that the sale achieved such results. In keeping with the wishes of the Duke and Duchess, as thanks to the nation that gave them a home, the proceeds were given to the Pasteur Institute for research into AIDS and cancer. ✄

Daisy Fellowes

4

Daisy Fellowes is acknowledged as having been one of the 20th century's most stylish and glamorous women – words that could equally well describe her jewelry collection. Named Marguerite Séverine Philippine, but always known as Daisy, she was born in Paris in 1890 into a world of wealth and privilege. Her mother, Isabelle Blanche Singer, was the daughter of the sewing-machine magnate Isaac Merritt Singer and her father was the 3rd Duc Decazes et de Glücksbierg. Owing to her mother's suicide in 1896, Daisy was brought up in France by her mother's sister Winnaretta, the wife of Prince Edmond de Polignac and a well-known patron of the arts, particularly music. Some accounts of Daisy's childhood, which report an open contempt for her appearance and a refusal to wash or even to comb her hair, seem at odds with the person *Vogue* later dubbed the best-dressed woman in the world.

In 1910, when she was 20, Daisy married Prince Jean de Broglie and they had three daughters: Emeline, Isabelle and Jacqueline. It was during the early years of this marriage that Daisy commissioned her portrait from a well-known society painter. The finished picture had a remarkable effect on her: she hated what she saw and from that moment decided to create a new Daisy, far removed from the plain and uninteresting person she saw staring back at her from the canvas. According to the Comte de La Moussaye, Daisy's grandson, she particularly disliked the line of her nose, which she immediately had reshaped, horrifyingly without the aid of an anaesthetic. She then bought a whole new wardrobe of clothes and changed her hairdresser. Perhaps more significantly, having the intelligence to realize the importance in life of a good knowledge of literature and the arts and her own lack of this social advantage, she immersed herself in books and visited museums and art galleries. In early 1918, de Broglie died in a military hospital in Algiers, a victim of the influenza pandemic.

Through her own efforts, Daisy had achieved a remarkable transformation and she was now regarded as one of the most elegant and fascinating women in Europe. It was therefore unsurprising that her period of widowhood was short-lived: in August 1919 she married the English financier the Hon. Reginald Fellowes, six years her senior. He was the second son of the 2nd Baron de Ramsey and, through his mother, Lady Rosamond Spencer-Churchill, he was a cousin of Winston Churchill and the 9th Duke of Marlborough. Although she was known for her numerous love affairs, Daisy was said to be devoted to Reginald. When he became ill and wheelchair-bound in later life, she was an attentive and caring wife. Reginald died in 1953.

The couple, together with their daughter, Rosamund, born in 1921, and Daisy's three daughters from her first marriage, moved between homes in various fashionable locations, including Les Zoraïdes, their villa on Cap Martin on the Riviera, where they hosted guests such as Winston Churchill, who enjoyed painting there. They spent idyllic days amid the orange groves and cypress trees, enjoying the views across to Monte Carlo where their yacht the *Sister Anne* was moored; the boat was the venue for many of their lavish parties and was lent to the Prince of Wales in 1935 for a cruise along the coast with Mrs Simpson.

In addition to their residence in Neuilly-sur-Seine, near Paris, in their later years the couple acquired Donnington Grove, an 18th-century gothic house with a landscaped park in Berkshire, where Daisy entertained her friends and kept a flock of black sheep. From the early 1920s Daisy became one of the uncrowned queens of the social scene and a leader of fashion. In James

Pope-Hennessy's account of Daisy, published in American *Vogue* in 1964 after her death, he commented that she had four major assets: great beauty, a subtle and barbed sense of humour, an inborn sense of dress, and a considerable fortune. Her hair, short or long, was usually sleeked back and her look was of elegant classicism, with no fuss or frills. Indeed, Cecil Beaton, who was a friend of long standing and took a number of photographs of her, said she had 'studied simplicity'. She will also be remembered as the beauty who wore black, not white, when presented at court; conveniently she found some obscure French cousin who had recently died as a valid reason for this unconventional attire. But Daisy was more than just a great hostess and fashion trendsetter, she was also Paris editor of *Harper's Bazaar* in the 1930s and wrote several novels.

Daisy had a passion for fine jewels; indeed, her collection was famous enough for reporters and fashion magazines to keep watch to see what amazing new jewel the stylish Mrs Fellowes would appear in next.

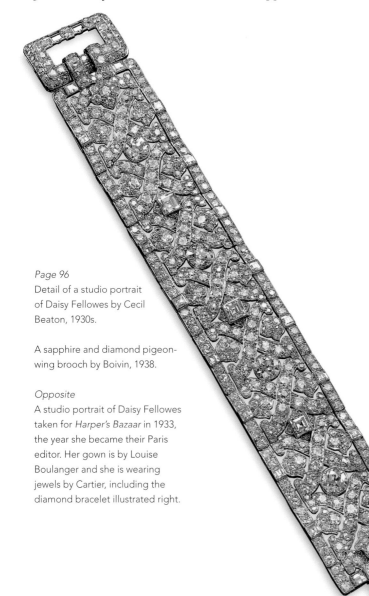

Page 96
Detail of a studio portrait of Daisy Fellowes by Cecil Beaton, 1930s.

A sapphire and diamond pigeon-wing brooch by Boivin, 1938.

Opposite
A studio portrait of Daisy Fellowes taken for *Harper's Bazaar* in 1933, the year she became their Paris editor. Her gown is by Louise Boulanger and she is wearing jewels by Cartier, including the diamond bracelet illustrated right.

However, tantalizingly few of her jewels have ever been sold at auction, so it is only from information supplied by her relations, together with articles, archive material and photographs that one can gain some knowledge of this outstanding collection.

Daisy Fellowes patronized many of the leading jewelers of her time, such as Cartier, Van Cleef & Arpels and Boivin. The incredibly long list of jewels that she acquired from Cartier confirms her stylish image. One of her most memorable acquisitions from that house was the 17.27 cts rose-pink diamond known as the 'Tête de Belier' (ram's head). This unusual stone, cut in the shape of a flattened octahedron, had been purchased by Cartier in 1927 from Prince Yusupov. It was thought to have been given by Catherine the Great to one of her favourites, Potemkin, who in turn gave it to his niece Princess Tatiana Yusupov, who was also the recipient of the 'Azra' pearl and acquired the 'Polar Star' diamond. The fashion designer Elsa Schiaparelli, whose clothes Daisy wore with panache, including the shoe hat, decided to commemorate the new addition to her client's collection – and to complement the colour of the stone – by creating the colour 'shocking pink' for her. In 1939, the diamond was stolen and its present location is one of the abiding mysteries of jewelry lore.

In 1921, Daisy Fellowes bought a very chic Cartier bracelet, typical of what became known as the Art Deco style. Based on a design by Charles Jacqueau and made by the Renault workshop for Cartier, Paris, the centre was a loop *pavé*-set with an oval cabochon emerald within a border of brilliant-cut diamonds. This was connected to the sides by two carved onyx hoops, linked to a three-row pearl bracelet. Some years later, Daisy had the onyx hoops removed and replaced with coral, and this is how it appeared when sold at auction in 1987 and again in 1989. Daisy's liking for the vibrant salmon pink colour of coral, more often than not combined with the rich green of emeralds and enhanced by diamonds, is also evident in a coral flowerhead brooch created by the firm of Cartier in the 1950s (p. 101). The carved coral petals are decorated with small pear-shaped emeralds and circular-cut diamonds.

Below
A Cartier chimera bangle in carved coral, diamonds and cabochon emeralds. It was ordered in December 1961, a year before Daisy Fellowes died.

Above
Two evening bags by Cartier, Paris, c. 1925. One clasp is set with turquoises, diamonds and black enamel, the other is set with coral, black enamel and diamonds. The ladybird brooch of coral, black enamel and diamonds was made by Cartier in the late 1930s.

A carved coral, diamond and emerald brooch in the form of a daisy, by Cartier, 1950s.

A necklace mounted by Cartier in the 1930s, composed of thirteen rows of graduated pearls, the clasp formed by a grey pearl in a cluster of diamonds, supporting two pearl drops and one coral drop, all three capped with diamonds.

A stylish necklace from the
1920s, designed to evoke a
waterfall. It is set with circular-cut
diamonds suspending seven
cabochon emerald drops. The
ring, probably by Boivin, has
a step-cut emerald within an
articulated bezel set with a fringe
of baguette diamonds, 1930s.

Opposite
Daisy photographed in London
in 1934 wearing her emerald and
diamond necklace together with
her Van Cleef & Arpels emerald
and diamond cuff bracelets.
In the *Tatler* in January 1935,
she was described as 'The
Quintessence of Chic'.

Two further diamonds form the anthers of the stamens. This brooch was also sold in the 1987 sale. Over the years Daisy bought many other coral jewels from Cartier, including two bracelets and a brooch with coral cylinders, which she commissioned from their Paris branch in 1932.

Late in 1961, Daisy showed her continuing love of coral by ordering a chimera bangle from Cartier, based on the ideas of Jeanne Toussaint (p. 100). Such bangles were originally produced in coral in 1922 and then in diamonds in 1929. Toussaint had instigated a new series in 1954, transforming the earlier, almost terrifying creatures (the mythical chimera was a combination of lion, goat and serpent) into rather more docile and appealing animals. Daisy's carved coral bangle had dolphin heads as the two terminals and the piece was decorated throughout with variously cut diamonds and emeralds.

In many photographs, Daisy Fellowes is seen wearing pearls, which she obviously loved, particularly in the form of bracelets and necklaces. In the 1930s, she had thirteen graduated rows of natural pearls mounted on a pearl and diamond clasp by Cartier (p. 101). The clasp was set with a grey pearl within a border of diamonds and had a pink coral drop between two pear-shaped pearl drops, capped by diamonds. The position of the clasp was such that it was worn at the nape of the neck, an elegant style very fashionable at that time.

Another stunning necklace from the 1920s that remained in Daisy's collection was designed as a waterfall cascade, set throughout with circular-cut diamonds supporting seven cabochon emerald drops (p. 102). In the same period she acquired some more unusual pieces, such as a bracelet made of panther skin that was set at the centre with a gemstone. In June 1938, she added one of Cartier's necklace/tiaras to her collection, the daisy design being a particularly appropriate choice. The three detachable flower-heads were set with diamonds and could also be worn as clips.

One of Daisy's innovations was wearing paired rings and cuffs – she regarded her hands and arms as unbalanced otherwise – and in the 1920s Van Cleef & Arpels provided her with two identical cuff bracelets in the 'Indian' style. The first was created in 1926 and its pair in 1929, and each was designed as a flexible wide band of baguette, marquise-shaped and

A pair of emerald and diamond cuff bracelets created for Daisy in 1926 and 1929 by Van Cleef & Arpels. The design for the 1929 bracelet is shown below.

Opposite
The two bracelets joined together as a choker necklace.

brilliant-cut diamonds set at intervals with larger step-cut diamonds, and both were fringed with articulated cabochon emerald drops. Mounted in platinum, the two bracelets could be converted into a choker necklace.

Daisy Fellowes was one of the best customers of Cartier's jewels in the Indian style and in 1936 she commissioned a sensational 'Hindou' necklace from the firm. In June 1928, she had bought from them a necklace of emerald and sapphire beads supporting a fringe of thirteen oval sapphire briolettes, capped by foliate platinum mounts set with brilliant-cut diamonds and with baguette diamond stems. A year later she acquired a bracelet of carved emerald buds decorated with diamond husks and ruby and turquoise bead tips, with carved ruby leaves and with two larger sapphires of 50.80 and 42.45 cts, carved as bud motifs. It was the stones from these pieces, apart from the small turquoise beads, along with those of another unidentified bracelet and nearly 250 extra stones from Cartier that Henri Lavabre used for the 'Collier Hindou' (p. 107), probably the most magnificent of the jewels the firm produced

in that style. The necklace was a graduated fringe of carved ruby, sapphire and emerald buds and foliage, the carved emerald buds forming a ruff, and the sapphire briolettes forming the fringe. The central section, which was also a detachable clip, was set with the two larger sapphire bud motifs. The necklace was fastened at the back by silk cords: this is a typically Indian method of fastening, which is still in use today as it gives the wearer complete flexibility to alter the length of the necklace, and hence the overall effect of the jewel.

In 1963, after Daisy's death, her eldest daughter, the Comtesse de Castéja, decided to alter the necklace and Cartier's expertise was sought once again. The silk cords were removed and the centre was redesigned: the two large carved sapphire buds became the clasp and the carved rubies and some of the emeralds were moved to the sides. It was in this form that it was sold at auction in 1991, achieving the highest price to that date for any Cartier jewel offered in the sale room. Cartier has no record of changes made to the necklace between 1936 and 1963, but Daisy had worn the necklace with the front in the form it was at the auction.

A studio portrait of Daisy by Cecil Beaton, taken in 1937. She is wearing the 'Hindou' necklace created for her by Cartier in 1936 (illustrated opposite). To make this extraordinary necklace, Daisy supplied almost all the stones originally set in a necklace dated 1928 and a bracelet from 1929, both from Cartier. The central motif could be detached and worn as a clip. In 1963, after Daisy's death, her eldest daughter, the Comtesse de Castéja, asked Cartier to remove the original silk thread used to fasten the necklace around the neck and had the removable clip unmounted in order to use the two large engraved sapphires and the other stones for the clasp. However, earlier photographs show Daisy wearing the necklace without the clip and with the front in its present form, so even without the clip the necklace could still be worn, probably by rotating the engraved square emeralds in the centre.

A photograph from the Cartier archives in Paris showing a diamond and engraved emerald tassel-drop clasp for a bead necklace of Indian inspiration, created by Cartier for Daisy in 1945. The two emeralds were originally set in a hatpin created for her by Cartier in 1939. In 1963, her eldest daughter, the Comtesse de Castéja, had the tassels mounted by Cartier as pendent earrings (opposite).

Above
Daisy photographed by Cecil
Beaton in her boudoir, 1941.

Far left and left
A sapphire and diamond brooch
by Boivin, designed as a stylized
pineapple set at the centre with
a foiled-back faceted sapphire,
c. 1940, and a yellow gold clip
designed as a tassel of corded
wire by Cartier, *c.* 1945.

Right
An archive photograph of a ruby bead necklace, *c.* 1939, with a gold, ruby and diamond thread and tassel clasp of Indian inspiration, originally mounted in Daisy's gem-set 'Tutti Frutti' necklace by Cartier (pp. 110–111) and later remounted on the same necklace, the ruby-bead string having undergone several alterations and the number of strings having been reduced from six to three. Once this clasp had been removed, the three strings were remounted in a simple yellow gold and diamond clasp.

A photograph by Cecil Beaton of Daisy in 1941 wearing her ruby bead necklace with gold, ruby and diamond tassels.

The 1938 'Tutti Frutti' Cartier necklace set with its original clasp, the design of which is preserved in the Cartier, Paris, archives. The necklace incorporates elements in the Indian style.

This is probably because the necklace was created to be worn with or without the central clip by rotating the two emeralds and removing the central sapphire briolette from the clip. Daisy wore this necklace, without the central clip, at the famous masked ball – the so-called 'Party of Parties' – hosted in Venice by the multi-millionaire Charles de Beistegui in 1951, and it has often been suggested that this was the only occasion on which she wore it. However, photographs by Cecil Beaton published by *Vogue* in January 1937 (p. 106) and elsewhere at other times show that Daisy wore the necklace to great effect more than that once.

At the 1991 auction where this necklace was sold, it was accompanied by a pair of pendent earrings (p. 107). Each earring was designed as a large emerald bead drop carved with floral motifs and with a diamond tip, capped by a calyx motif set with diamonds and suspended from a flowerhead cluster surmount, set with a diamond-studded emerald bead within a border of diamonds. These carved emerald drops and the calyx motifs had originally been in a brooch owned by Daisy.

In 1939, she ordered Cartier to use them to create a hatpin. Later, in 1945, the firm mounted the two emeralds as the tassel drops for a gold chain and diamond clasp for a two-row bead necklace, as recorded in a photograph from the Cartier archives (p. 106). This style of clasp was probably the inspiration for the necklace created by Cartier for the Duchess of Windsor in 1949 (see p. 70). The emeralds became the pendants of the pair of emerald and diamond earrings in 1963, at the wish of the Comtesse de Castéja.

According to Daisy's youngest daughter, Rosamund, the more traditional ladylike jewels bored the stylish socialite, and her passion for multi-coloured gem-set necklaces is shown in another carved coloured stone and diamond 'Tutti Frutti' necklace from Cartier (p. 111). She acquired it in 1938 and the original design is preserved in the Cartier archives in Paris. The dramatic fringe of carved flowerheads, foliage and buds was decorated with diamonds and was surmounted by Indian flowerhead clusters beneath a row of beads. Again, the fastener was cord, but this time made from

A panther clip brooch by Cartier, 1950s, the design inspired by the badge of the Order of the Golden Fleece. The articulated head, legs and tail are *pavé*-set with single-cut diamonds; the spots are cabochon sapphires.

Below
A ring by Suzanne Belperron, *c.* 1930s, collet-set with a circular cabochon sapphire in a circular-cut diamond *pavé* accented with circular cabochon sapphires.

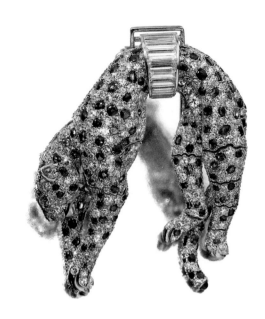

gold wire, the slide set with *calibré*-cut rubies and the looped tassels decorated with a diamond band. This same gold fastener with its gem-set decorations was later reused for various ruby bead necklaces (p. 109); the final version of six rows, connected to the cord fastener by diamond calyx motifs, was commissioned by her in July 1939 and later reset in the 'Tutti Frutti' necklace.

In the 1940s, Daisy's many purchases from Cartier included an exquisite sapphire, emerald and diamond brooch designed as an iris, made in the firm's London workshop. The petals were set with cushion-shaped sapphires and brilliant-cut diamonds, the emerald stem entwined with baguette diamonds.

Like many of her contemporaries, Daisy admired the 'Great Cat' jewels that were the inspiration of Jeanne Toussaint, director of fine jewelry at Cartier. In the 1950s, Daisy commissioned a panther brooch in sapphires and diamonds modelled on the gold badge of the Order of the Golden Fleece, an order of chivalry founded by Philip the Good, Duke of Burgundy, in 1430. Toussaint substituted a highly realistic jewelled leopard hanging from a band of baguette diamonds for the ram's fleece (above).

Daisy's choice of jewels from the talented designers at Boivin revealed in particular her great admiration for their spectacular brooches. Based in Paris, the house of Boivin was founded by René Boivin in the late 19th century. Upon his death in 1917, when he was only 53, the business was carried on by his equally gifted wife, Jeanne, the eldest sister of the couturier Paul Poiret.

Daisy photographed by Cecil Beaton in the 1920s and (below) a magnificent iris brooch by Cartier, c. 1940. The petals are set with cushion-shaped sapphires highlighted with cushion-shaped, circular-cut and baguette diamonds. The stem is set with step-cut emeralds.

A sapphire and diamond bracelet, 1930s, designed as a series of arched links set with circular-cut and rose diamonds. The clasp is collet-set with a foiled-back octagonal mixed-cut sapphire.

Preceding pages
Daisy Fellowes photographed by
Cecil Beaton in 1951 at the masked
ball hosted by Charles de Beistegui at
the Palazzo Labia in Venice (left). Her
costume by Dior represented early
18th-century America. She is wearing
her Cartier 'Hindou' necklace of 1936
and a pair of gem-set bracelets by
Suzanne Belperron, created for her
in 1939 (right).

A gem-set butterfly brooch,
probably by Boivin and designed
by Suzanne Belperron, mid-1930s.
The articulated upper wings are
set with variously cut citrines and
the lower wings are *pavé*-set with
circular-cut diamonds and step-
cut emeralds. The body is set with
blue enamel and a cabochon ruby,
with a step-cut emerald for the
head. The antennae are set with
cabochon pear-shaped emeralds.

Opposite
Daisy Fellowes with the Marchese
Strozzi at a gala evening at the
Monte Carlo Sporting Club in
1937. She is wearing the butterfly
brooch.

Mme Boivin, a highly innovative designer and an astute business woman, engaged several aspiring young designers, including Suzanne Belperron and Juliette Moutard, as well as her own daughter Germaine, and the company went from strength to strength, admired for the imaginative sculptural style of its creations. Very few of the firm's pieces were signed as Mme Boivin felt that a beautiful jewel did not require a signature and regarded its addition as 'pure affectation'. Signatures were added only if the client insisted.

Daisy Fellowes became one of Boivin's most important clients, sometimes acquiring several jewels at one time. Boivin's records show that in March 1939 she ordered an orchid, a daffodil ring, a chameleon, a pair of earrings, a daisy, an arrow and two tourmaline leaves. Apart from the chameleon brooch, every other design was a new creation from Boivin. In 1991, one especially dramatic example from Daisy's collection came up for auction. It was impressive not only for its design but also for its size: designed as the wing of a pigeon, it was almost 13 cms in width (p. 96). *Pavé*-set with cabochon sapphires and baguette and circular-cut diamonds, it had a distinct feeling of movement, which only a truly skilled craftsman can achieve, and was created by Boivin in 1938. The Comte de La Moussaye, son of Daisy's daughter Isabelle, recounts that some of these sapphires were acquired by Daisy in what was then Ceylon during one of her voyages aboard the *Sister Anne* and that she spent many hours on the sun-drenched deck musing as to which jewel the stones should embellish.

Another of her wonderful brooches, although again unsigned, bears all the hallmarks of these creative jewelers. The design is that of a huge butterfly, its upper wings set with citrines of various cuts and sizes and the lower wings *pavé*-set with emeralds and diamonds (p. 116). The body was decorated with blue enamel and set with a cabochon ruby, the head with a step-cut emerald and the antennae with two pear-shaped emeralds. There was also a stylish sapphire and diamond pineapple brooch that did bear Boivin's marks (p. 108). The large foiled-back faceted sapphire was close-set at the centre of a gold scrolled border, surrounded by diamonds and surmounted by a diamond foliate motif.

Other Boivin jewels in Daisy's collection included a large grey enamel and diamond whelk brooch and a

ruby and diamond orchid brooch. She also had a pair of colourful bracelets set with a variety of cabochon gemstones (p. 115), created for her in 1939 by Suzanne Belperron, which she wore at the Beistegui ball in 1951 with her Cartier 'Hindou' necklace. Her collection was further enhanced with jewels by the talented French designer Jean Schlumberger, who later worked for Tiffany. A piece of particular note was a clip from the late 1940s set with a large cabochon amethyst in the shape of a plum. The carved peridot leaf was set with cabochon rubies and brilliant-cut diamonds and surmounted by a frond of turquoise.

When Daisy Fellowes died in December 1962 at her *hôtel particulier* in the rue de Lille in Paris, just behind what is now the Musée d'Orsay, Graham Sutherland was completing her portrait. Although she was then in her early seventies – and had quarrelled with half of Paris, according to Nancy Mitford – James Pope-Hennessy thought that the portrait conveyed a sense of Daisy's disciplined serenity and an inkling of her grand allure. The contrast with her own reaction to her first portrait could not have been more marked. She had indeed fashioned herself, as she had wished, into a living work of art. ※

Countess Mona Bismarck

5

The jewelry collection of Mona Bismarck demonstrated her love of beautiful gemstones, as well as her devotion to the luxurious pursuits of life. Unlike many of her famous contemporaries, Mona did not come from a background of wealth or high social standing, but she did have the beauty and intelligence that enabled her to acquire them.

Born Mona Travis Strader in Louisville, Kentucky, in 1897, she had been twice married and divorced by the age of 27. The first marriage, in 1917, to wealthy businessman Henry Schlesinger, prompted a move to Milwaukee, where she gave birth to a son, Robert. The second marriage was to a rich banker, James Irving Bush, also from Milwaukee, said to be the handsomest man in America. After this, too, failed, in 1924, Mona settled in New York, where she revelled in the world of high society. She soon met Harrison Williams, a widower twenty-four years her senior, who had become one of the richest men in America through his investments in public utilities. The couple married in 1926 and embarked on a round-the-world cruise on his steam yacht, the *Warrior*. When they returned, Mona was in her element in the fashionable and wealthy circles to which her husband belonged.

As well as moving into a neo-Georgian mansion on upper Fifth Avenue in New York (built for Willard Straight in 1915), the Williamses acquired Oak Point, a huge property at Bayville on the north shore of Long Island. In addition to a 25-room house, the estate had its own golf course, and the couple added a sports pavilion that featured a tennis court and a swimming pool. In 1927, Mona commissioned the Catalan muralist José Maria Sert to paint three frescoes for the tennis court. Her taste in art could be seen elsewhere – the walls of the New York home were graced with paintings by Goya, Tiepolo and Fragonard, and she employed Syrie Maugham to decorate that house and the Williamses' villa in Palm Beach, where the colourful Chinese wallpaper in the salon features in a sketch of the couple by Cecil Beaton, painted in 1937.

Mona became a lifelong friend – and photographic subject – of Beaton's. His studio portraits of her were classical yet inspired, often showing her dressed in creations by the most popular couturiers of the time. He described her as 'one of the few outstanding beauties of the thirties … who represented the epitome of all that taste and luxury can bring to flower.' She was also soon sought-out by other prominent photographers of the period, such as Edward Steichen and Horst.

By the early 1930s, Mona's beauty and elegance were a subject of note on both sides of the Atlantic. In 1933, she was voted the best-dressed woman in the world in the annual poll held by the major French couture houses. Cole Porter, in the song 'Ridin' High', sung by Ethel Merman in his musical *Red, Hot and Blue* (1936), picked up on the prevailing mood: 'What do I care if Mrs Harrison Williams is the best-dressed woman in town?'

In the numerous photographic portraits of Mona taken in the late 1920s and 1930s, her beauty is enhanced by her stylish period jewels. Like many of her contemporaries, she had her jewels redesigned to keep up with the fashion, so only a few of her Art Deco pieces survive in their original form. One such piece is a circular brooch by Cartier in jade, onyx and rubies, reminiscent of the Oriental style popular in that period (p. 118).

A photograph of Mona by Beaton, published in 1938 (p. 121), shows her wearing emerald and diamond jewels dating from the 1920s. Once their style became dated, she had the pieces redesigned (p. 120). The first to be altered was an emerald and diamond bangle. The central carved emerald and diamond flowerhead motif became the clasp of a bracelet strung with seven rows of natural pearls. In the 1960s, two carved emeralds, formerly set in two clips, were remounted as the drops for an extremely elegant brooch by Cartier, Paris. These pear-shaped emeralds, carved with flowerheads and foliage, were capped by diamonds and suspended from a ribbon bow of baguette and brilliant-cut diamonds.

In the same photograph of 1938, Mona is wearing a large emerald ring carved with motifs similar to those on the emerald drops. Again in the late 1960s, she had this rectangular emerald remounted and set at the centre of a bracelet. It was placed between two leaves, *pavé*-set with diamonds and bordered by green enamel, and the back was composed of two rows of emerald beads connected by diamond rondels, originally sections of another 1920s jewel.

Left and far left
A carved emerald and diamond *negligé* brooch by Cartier, Paris, and an emerald and diamond bracelet. Mona Bismarck had the stones remounted in this form in the 1960s. The two carved emerald drops from the brooch were originally mounted as clips and the central carved emerald rectangular plaque from the bracelet was formerly set in a ring. The clips and the ring can be seen in the Beaton photograph of Mona taken by Cecil Beaton for *Vogue* in 1938 (opposite).

Below
A pearl, carved emerald and diamond bracelet. The carved emerald and diamond flowerhead clasp was originally the centrepiece of a stylish bangle, as can be seen in the Beaton photograph opposite. Once again, this was one of the jewels that Mona had altered at a later date, probably by Cartier.

Page 118
Mona Williams (later Countess Mona Bismarck), photographed by Cecil Beaton.

A stylish jade, onyx and ruby Art Deco brooch/pendant by Cartier.

A late 19th-century ruby and diamond necklace of foliate and cluster design by Boucheron; a ruby and diamond cluster ring and earrings; a pair of ruby and diamond bracelets by Petochi, 1950s; a brooch with a step-cut ruby of 36.36 cts in a brilliant-cut diamond cluster.

Opposite
Mona photographed by Cecil Beaton in 1938 with one of her pet dogs; a passion of hers.

Left
Mona, photographed by Cecil Beaton in 1936, wearing her aquamarine *parure* by Suzanne Belperron.

Above
Cabochon emerald and diamond ear clips created in the late 1940s by Cartier, Paris.

Opposite
Two evening bags by Cartier, Paris, late 1920s. The top one has a frame set with black and red enamel on a circular-cut diamond ground; its handle is similarly decorated, supporting an onyx, coral and pearl tassle. The second bag has a frame set with black enamel and circular-cut diamonds; its clasp is formed by a carved emerald of barrel shape.

Mona wore these emerald jewels with a stunning 1920s evening bag created by Cartier, its platinum frame completely set with a diamond and black enamel motif, its clasp formed of a cabochon carved emerald. She had another bag by Cartier of the same date. For this one the diamonds were united with an onyx, coral and pearl tassle, to great effect (p. 125).

Beaton described Mona as having 'a fascinating beauty, like a rock crystal deity with aquamarine eyes'. A 1936 photograph (above) by him shows Mona wearing a parure set with this gemstone; the necklace, of bib design, was set with step-cut aquamarines and the large matching bracelet was set with various cuts of the stone. These stylish jewels, along with a matching ring, were the creation of Suzanne Belperron, the most fashionable designer of the period, whom Mona – as well as most of the grandes dames of her time – liked to patronize. This set appeared in an auction in Geneva in 1980, sadly with no provenance. There are two other jewels from the 1920s and 1930s that survive: a 'black and white' diamond and black-bead bracelet, its geometric design and bold colour combination typical of the Art Deco period, and another bracelet composed of five rows of jade beads connected at intervals by diamond rondels. Its diamond clasp was set at the centre with a jade plaque carved in the form of a finger citron with a small spider (p. 134).

Another stunning jewel is her sapphire and diamond necklace by Cartier, which she donated to the Smithsonian Institution in Washington, DC, in 1967. It features a magnificent 98.57 cts Burmese cushion-shaped sapphire, accented with eight square-cut sapphires. The stone is set at the centre of a clip that can be unmounted from the baguette and brilliant-cut diamond necklace and worn as a brooch. The sapphire is now known as the 'Bismarck Sapphire' (p. 127).

Opposite
Mona, photographed by
Horst in the 1930s, wearing
sapphire jewels.

A sapphire and diamond
necklace by Cartier, set at
the centre with a magnificent
98.57 cts Burmese cushion-
shaped sapphire. The central
motif could be detached and
used as a clip brooch. Mona
Bismarck donated the necklace
to the Smithsonian in 1967.

An antique diamond festoon
necklace. The briolette diamonds
and the pendent clasp are a later
addition. The total weight of the
diamonds is almost 90 cts.

Right
An informal photograph of Mona
with her friend Cecil Beaton.

Below
Mona, photographed by Horst
for *Vogue*, wearing two gold and
diamond brooches designed
by Suzanne Belperron. The
sculpted matt-finished gold
peppers with diamond stems
were identical to the brooch
illustrated below right. In the
same studio portrait, Mona is
wearing her carved emerald
ring and her jade and diamond
bracelet (p. 134).

Although Mona's jewelry collection reflected an apparent willingness to conform to the trends of the day, it also showed that she had her own individual sense of style that rose above the vagaries of fashion. Many of the most important jewels in her collection either originated in the 19th century or were created for her in that style. A stunning example of her period jewelry was a ruby and diamond necklace in a design of foliate and cluster motifs. When it was sold at the Sotheby's sale in Geneva in 1986, after Mona's death, the origin of this elegant necklace was unknown, but a book on the Boucheron archives published in 2009 revealed that the necklace was made by this prestigious French firm in 1888 for Marie Louise Mackay, the wife of John Mackay, whose incredible fortune came from a silver mine that he owned in Nevada.

In the 1950s, the jeweler Petochi of Rome created for Mona a pair of bracelets from rubies and old-cut diamonds in a 19th-century style, which could be worn with the necklace. Over the years she acquired a ruby and diamond cluster ring, earrings and an impressive brooch, set with a step-cut ruby of 36.36 cts, simply mounted in a brilliant-cut diamond cluster, to complete the ensemble (p. 123).

Another late 19th-century piece in Mona's collection was a sensational serpent necklace that she wore coiled around her neck. The reptile is realistically enamelled and its diamond head is capped by a pearl (right). Another jewel of the same period was the diamond festoon necklace designed as a simple *rivière* of variously shaped old-cut diamonds, supporting detachable garlands and drops, which were all mounted in silver collets backed by gold (p. 128). Since it was first made, the piece had been altered, including the addition of two diamond briolette drops (the third and fifth of the seven stones along the bottom edge) and a four-stone pendant hanging from the clasp, an embellishment that Mona added to most of her necklaces.

The grandeur and design of that necklace appealed to her, and elements of the style were incorporated in the necklace created for her by Cartier in the 1940s. The *rivière* of twenty-four circular-cut diamonds in this necklace was embellished with two briolette diamond drops hanging from the clasp (p. 132). The stones were graduated in size from the front, the largest

An antique enamel, pearl and diamond serpent necklace.

A pair of pearls in a cluster of old-cut diamonds by Chantecler Capri.

A pearl and diamond pendant set at the centre with a button-shaped pearl measuring 19.20 mm in diameter in a border of cushion-shaped diamonds.

Opposite
Mona, photographed by Beaton, wearing the serpent necklace.

A diamond *rivière* necklace by Cartier, Paris, together with a pair of diamond solitaire ear clips and a matching diamond bracelet. The back of the necklace is decorated by a *negligé* diamond motif supporting two briolette diamonds weighing together approximately 12 cts. Mona had a penchant for adding this kind of stylish drop motif at the back of her necklaces. The central stone weighs 16.45 cts and the total weight of the diamonds in this *parure* is almost 170 cts.

Opposite
A diamond bracelet by Cartier, designed with two rows of old-cut diamonds, set at the centre with a marquise-shaped diamond of approximately 9 cts.

Right
A diamond ring by Cartier, set with a step-cut stone weighing 31.77 cts, the shoulders set with baguette diamonds.

weighing approximately 16.45 cts and the smallest just over 2 cts. This necklace was complemented by a matching bracelet and ear clips. The centre of the bracelet was set with a stone of over 18 cts and the whole *parure* was mounted in platinum and yellow gold.

Cartier created another splendid diamond bracelet for Mona that was based on 19th-century designs. The centre of this piece was set with a large marquise-shaped diamond of nearly 9 cts within an oval border of cushion-shaped stones connected to two graduated rows of similarly shaped stones (below). The highlight of the 1986 sale, however, was the diamond ring by Cartier set with a step-cut stone of the finest D colour, weighing 31.77 cts (p. 132). This one jewel encapsulates Mona's desire for perfection and beauty.

Emeralds featured in her collection and one of her most cherished sets was an emerald and diamond necklace and cluster ear clips by Cartier, which recreated the stylish designs of the previous century, with old-cut diamonds decorating the emeralds (p. 135). Cartier also provided her with a five-row pearl bracelet, the diamond clasp centred by a step-cut emerald (p. 138), and a stunning pair of diamond earrings set with two large pear-shaped cabochon emeralds and unusually mounted, not as a pendant but instead protruding upwards in double loops of graduated old-cut diamonds (p. 124). The finest emerald in her collection, however, was another step-cut stone, weighing approximately 10 cts, set in a delicate early 20th-century ring within a double-row border of old-cut diamonds.

During the 1930s Mona and Harrison Williams took annual cruises on the *Warrior* and visited exotic locations such as India, China and Iraq. On one such trip, Mona fell in love with the island of Capri. She was captivated by the beautiful landscape, the lush vegetation and the crystal-blue sea. Famous since Roman times, the island was a favourite spot of the Emperor Tiberius, who had several villas there. Built on the ruins of one of these, and originally a Spanish fortress, was a villa called Il Fortino, which Harrison bought for Mona. Over the years she purchased more land around the property and created one of the most exquisite gardens on the island with terraces full of colourful and scented flowers. There, comfortably dressed and wearing a big straw hat to protect her from the sun, she used to garden; in the late 1960s Beaton captured her dressed this way in her rose garden for *Vogue*. Mona became well known for the botanical knowledge she gained in creating this island paradise.

The villa on Capri was not the only property acquired by the Williamses in the early 1930s. They also took possession of an apartment in the fabled Hôtel Lambert – where Chopin had composed – on the Île St Louis in Paris. They were a celebrated and much admired couple, whose circle included monarchs and exiled royalty, statesmen, tycoons, film stars, writers and artists. Truman Capote is said to have based a character in his unfinished novel *Answered Prayers* on Mona and in 1943 Salvador Dalí painted her portrait. Beaton summed it all up: 'her houses, her furniture, her jewelry, her way of life were little short of a tour de force.'

Mona, in keeping with her generation, had a passion for pearls. 'By day,' wrote Diana Vreeland, 'I never saw her without her enormous pearls gleaming on her immaculate skin.' The most magnificent of her pearl jewels was a two-row necklace. Strung with 37 and 33 pearls, the two rows were graduated in size from 7.7 mm to 15 mm and had a diamond clasp (p. 138). For natural pearls, their size, lustre and colour were superb. They were matched by a pair of 17.25-mm pearl and diamond ear clips by Petochi of Rome.

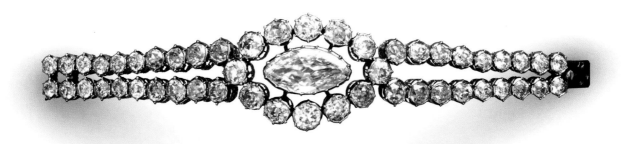

Mona, photographed in Paris by Cecil Beaton in 1958 (opposite). She is wearing her emerald and diamond cluster necklace and ear clips by Cartier, Paris (above). On her right arm is her jade and diamond bracelet (opposite below) and on her left wrist her pearl bracelet with emerald and diamond clasp (p. 138).

Another important pearl necklace was composed of a single row of 27 pearls, graduated from 13.8 mm to 10.8 mm. Mona had also bought an elegant pair of button-pearl and diamond-cluster ear clips by Chantecler, the noted jewelers from Capri (p. 131). Each of the pearls, approximately 16 mm in diameter, was mounted within a border of cushion-shaped diamonds. In her collection, there were many other equally desirable jewels that were less formal than her grandest *parures*, such as an elegant turquoise necklace, designed as a *résille* (or net), the trellis decorated with seed pearls, circular turquoises and rose diamonds supporting a fringe of pear-shaped turquoises capped by diamonds. She loved to wear it with several pearl bracelets.

Mona Bismarck's passion for pearls continued over the years. From Cartier came a two-row pearl bracelet, the clasp set with three old-cut diamonds, entwined by a looped border of brilliant-cut diamonds. Mona's choice of these jewels set with cushion-shaped diamonds, rather than modern brilliant-cuts, provides further evidence of her preference for older styles and her individual taste. Her other pearl jewels, all embellished with diamonds, included a stylish hat pin from the 1920s, a chandelier brooch (p. 138) and a pendant set with a spectacular button pearl 19.20 mm in diameter (p. 131).

The Williamses spent the Second World War in the United States. Even for someone as wealthy as Harrison, the depression of the 1930s had left its mark. At Oak Point they gave up the big house (it was torn down in 1950) and transformed the sports pavilion into their home, filling in the swimming pool and converting the tennis court into an aviary. After a long illness, Harrison died at Oak Point in 1953 at the age of 80 and Mona inherited a vast fortune.

The following year, she married Count Edward von Bismarck, grandson of the famous chancellor of Germany. He had acted as secretary to the couple and with his skill as an interior decorator helped with restoring Il Fortino, damaged in the war. Mona and he moved to Europe permanently and in 1956 she bought a mansion in Paris at 34 Avenue de New York, which she completely redecorated.

Mona was a glamorous and well-liked hostess in Paris and on Capri, entertaining guests such as the Duke and Duchess of Windsor, Churchill, Onassis and Maria Callas. She was always resplendent in her jewels

Above and right
A turquoise, pearl and diamond *résille* necklace. The photograph shows Mona wearing the necklace, in the company of the Duke and Duchess of Windsor, at the Lido cabaret in Paris in December 1962. Her tulle dress, embroidered in turquoise, was created by her favourite designer, Balenciaga, to match the necklace.

Opposite
Mona photographed by Cecil Beaton in Paris in 1958. The purple lace gown was by Balenciaga, whom she patronized until he retired in 1968.

Mona, photographed in a Balenciaga gown by Cecil Beaton in the Hôtel Lambert, Paris, in 1955, playing with her pet dogs.

Opposite (from the top)
An important two-row pearl necklace, graduated from 7.7 to 15 mm, the clasp collet-set with a large cushion-shaped diamond in a cluster of diamonds.

A pearl and diamond chandelier brooch.

A pair of ear clips by Petochi, each one set with a pearl approximately 17.25 mm in diameter surmounted with a cushion-shaped diamond.

A five-strand pearl bracelet by Cartier, Paris. The clasp is collet-set with a large step-cut emerald, weighing almost 12 cts, in a diamond border.

and beautiful dresses by Cristóbal Balenciaga, which were the perfect backdrop for her jewelry. After he retired in 1968, she transferred her loyalty to Hubert de Givenchy and she is said to have been buried on Long Island in one of his dresses.

After the death of Count Bismarck in 1970, Mona had an unhappy marriage to Umberto de Martini, who died in a car accident in 1979. Her last years were spent quietly and she died at her Paris home in 1983, at the age of 86. Her legacy continues in a foundation that bears her name, based in her mansion in Paris, which fosters Franco-American friendship through art and culture. The proceeds of the 1986 auction of her jewels went to support the foundation. Those gems were as beautiful and memorable as Mona herself. ✂

Barbara Hutton

6

When Barbara Hutton died in 1979, she reportedly left very little money, but the probated will revealed that she had retained many of her most important jewels. Among her bequests were the fabulous 'Pasha' diamond, a spectacular suite of rubies and diamonds, and various pearl and diamond pieces. As only a few of her most famous jewels have appeared in the salerooms since 1985, it is tantalizing to try and discover the full extent of her collection.

Barbara Woolworth Hutton was born in New York City on 14 November 1912, the daughter of Edna and Franklyn Hutton and the granddaughter of Frank Winfield Woolworth, founder of the phenomenally successful chain of retail stores bearing his name. At the age of four, she was to discover the body of her mother who, it was reported in the press, had died of complications caused by a chronic ear ailment. There was no mention of Franklyn Hutton's womanizing or of the police reports that an empty vial of poison was found in Edna's bathroom. Frank Woolworth had been aware of his daughter's unhappiness and had attempted to persuade her to start divorce proceedings, as well as trying to stop his son-in-law's philandering. Whatever the circumstances of Edna's death, it was not made the subject of further investigation.

For the next two years, until he died in April 1919, Barbara was cared for by her grandfather at Winfield Hall in Glen Cove, Long Island. Thereafter, her life became even more unsettled as she was moved from one relative to another, her father always ready with material but not emotional support. This disorganized start to her life obviously had a strong impact on her as an adult. The only constant appears to have been the vast fortune she inherited from her grandparents and her mother: before she was in her teens, she had well over $28 million in trust, and this was to be nearly doubled by the time she came of age. She partied, travelled and lived a life of excessive excitement and self-indulgence, a pattern that was set from then on. She was always a 'poor little rich girl', the title of a Noël Coward song of 1925, forever seeking love and contentment, which resulted in seven short marriages. By the end of her life, ill and with her wealth greatly diminished, she had become a virtual recluse.

The last years were in sharp contrast to her glamorous launch in society some fifty years earlier. Her debut was held in December 1930, the first year of the Depression, an economic disaster from which Barbara was shielded by sound investments. Her coming-out was in three stages: a tea party for 500 at the triplex on Fifth Avenue belonging to her uncle Edward Hutton and his wife, Marjorie Merriweather Post; a dinner and dance at the Central Park Casino, also for 500 guests; and a ball at the Ritz-Carlton Hotel on Madison Avenue that cost some $60,000. Her aunt Marjorie disapproved of Barbara's lavish lifestyle and tried to convince her that in difficult times such public displays of wealth were not appropriate, but to no avail. Marjorie's instinct was right – these events generated so much criticism that Barbara was scared to go out alone. Nor did the gatherings produce appropriate suitors; decent men steered clear of her and she was prey to playboys and fortune hunters. To boost his daughter's marriage chances, Franklyn Hutton took Barbara to London, where in May 1931 she was presented at court to King George V and Queen Mary.

Hutton's efforts were in vain. Barbara had already met Alexis Mdivani, a Russian emigré of questionable nobility and one of five siblings who were known as the 'marrying Mdivanis'. Marjorie told Barbara that the Mdivani brothers were 'bad news'. Nonetheless,

141

Barbara Hutton's jade bead
necklace, mounted with a ruby
and diamond clasp by Cartier,
1933, and her ruby and diamond
ring, created by Cartier in 1934
to match the necklace.

Barbara's relationship with the prince continued and the couple were married in Paris in 1933. A civil ceremony was held on 20 June and the religious ceremony took place two days later at the Russian Orthodox Cathedral of St Alexander Nevsky in the rue Daru. For the first, the bride wore a pale grey outfit by Chanel to complement her black pearl engagement ring, created by Cartier; and for the church ceremony she chose an ivory satin gown. She commissioned Cartier to design a somewhat unusual tiara reminiscent of those she had seen on a trip to Bali. It was made of tortoiseshell decorated with delicate diamond trefoil motifs, a design that was echoed in the lace veil. Thousands of Parisians crowded outside the church to see the heiress and the hundreds of official guests included Daisy Fellowes, resplendent in two large cuff bracelets of Indian inspiration by Van Cleef & Arpels.

The presents received by the bride included several exquisite pieces of jewelry. From a young age, Barbara displayed a great passion for gemstones, and especially for jade of the jadeite variety, having been introduced to it by the owner of Gump's, the San Francisco shop that specialized in Oriental artefacts. Although the majority of her vast collection was ornamental objects, she did have some amazing jade jewels. It is believed that both her father and Alexis Mdivani gave her jade

Barbara with her first husband, Prince Alexis Mdivani, photographed in 1933 at the Metropolitan Opera House in New York. She is wearing her jade necklace and the ruby and diamond bracelet of French manufacture illustrated at right.

Page 140
Barbara Hutton, photographed by Cecil Beaton at Sidi Hosni, her palace in Tangier, in 1961. She is wearing the Vladimir emeralds as a tiara together with the Marie Antoinette pearl necklace.

'The Spirit of Beauty Fairy Brooch', by Van Cleef & Arpels, set in diamonds, emeralds and rubies, with wings in rose diamonds. It was bought by Barbara in 1944.

necklaces. In 1988, an important jade bead necklace from the estate of Princess Nina Mdivani, Alexis's sister, was auctioned in Geneva. The catalogue described it as 'one of the most splendid jade necklaces (of the jadeite variety) for size and colour to have been offered on the international market.' It consisted of a row of 27 large jade beads of beautiful translucency and a brilliant green colour, graduated from 15 to 19 mm, with a ruby and diamond clasp (p. 142). This was probably one of Barbara's wedding presents from her father. Records in Cartier's Paris archives reveal that in 1933 the necklace was insured for $55,000 and left with the French firm, at which point the elegant ruby and diamond clasp was added. In 1934, Cartier created a jade, ruby and diamond ring to match the necklace.

Of all the pieces of jewelry that Barbara received at her wedding, the most impressive was also from her father. Bought from Cartier, it was a necklace of 53 pearls that had been worn by Marie Antoinette, Queen of France. This jewel, which the press described as 'one of the rarest strands of pearls ever sold by Cartier', became one of Barbara's most cherished possessions;

Opposite
Detail of a studio portrait of
Barbara Hutton by Horst, New
York, 1939. She is wearing the
Marie Antoinette pearl necklace.

Right
The historically important
necklace of pearls that had
formerly been worn by Marie
Antoinette, Queen of France.
Bought from Cartier, Paris, this
jewel was given to Barbara by
her father as a wedding present
on the occasion of her marriage
to Prince Alexis Mdivani in 1933.
Cartier later created a black opal
and diamond clasp, on Barbara's
instruction.

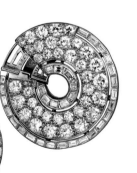

Barbara with her second husband, Count Kurt von Haugwitz-Reventlow, at the christening of their son, Lance, together with Barbara's father, Franklyn Hutton. The ceremony took place in the private chapel at Marlborough House, London, on 12 June 1936. Barbara is wearing a pair of diamond disc ear clips by Van Cleef & Arpels, created in 1935 when she was still the Princess Mdivani. The original design is shown on the far left.

Opposite
An emerald and diamond bracelet by Cartier, 1935. It was commissioned by Count Henrik Haugwitz-Reventlow using the family emeralds and given to Barbara Hutton shortly after her marriage to his brother.

she wore it during the day and at night, and had its length adjusted according to the vagaries of fashion. When it was sold in 1992, the necklace comprised 40 pearls, but Cartier's records confirmed that it had been restrung and altered many times for their valued client.

This extravagant wedding present was the beginning of Barbara's passion for pearls. One of her social secretaries, Mona Eldridge, recalled not only those famous white pearls but also a necklace of two strings of golden pearls and an equally remarkable row of black pearls. Matching earrings obviously accompanied these necklaces, much like the ones by Bulgari that appeared in an international sale in 1980, set with two natural pearls – one white and one black – in a double cluster of pear-shaped diamonds (p. 148). An important golden cultured pearl necklace was auctioned in London in 1988 with the provenance of the Princess Nina Mdivani (p. 152); it is probable that this necklace was given in later years by Barbara to her former sister-in-law.

The white pearl necklace was sold as 'the property of a member of a European Noble Family, formerly from the collection of Barbara Hutton.' It had not been Franklyn Hutton's first purchase for his daughter at Cartier. In the summer of 1929 he persuaded the reluctant Barbara to accompany him on a trip to Europe by offering her a jewel of her choice. Apparently when they called in at Cartier in New York trays of magnificent ruby rings were brought out for her to inspect. Once Barbara had made her choice the salesman beamed but her father was less ecstatic: the ruby she had chosen was the finest in Cartier's stock and cost Hutton $50,000, ten times the figure he had envisaged spending. At least he was assured of his daughter's impeccable taste in jewels.

Barbara became a fervent admirer of Cartier's jewels, and made many purchases from the firm. The ruby ring was the beginning of a lifelong passion for that stone. Several photographs from the 1930s show the heiress wearing a sumptuous ruby and diamond *fin de siècle résille* necklace. Later, she had this piece remounted, probably by Cartier, as a necklace/tiara with an exotic motif of lotus flowers. In addition, she possessed a pair of matching bracelets and ear clips.

Both friends and jewelers observed that Barbara not only loved her jewels and gems but was also very knowledgeable about them. She was said to be so fascinated by the jewels that she would spend many hours holding, studying and admiring each piece, not as an object of commercial value but as a beautiful combination of nature's and man's creation. She loved important gemstones, but she also liked light and elegant designs, such as the two platinum and diamond ribbon brooches that she acquired in 1934 from Van Cleef & Arpels.

In May 1935, Barbara's first marriage ended in divorce in Reno, Nevada, twenty-four hours after which she married the Prussian-born Danish Count Kurt Haugwitz-Reventlow, with whom she had her only child, Lance, born in 1936. At the christening in June that year, at Marlborough House in London, she wore a pair of diamond disc ear clips by Van Cleef & Arpels – a design that was very much in fashion in that period. Wallis Simpson had a similar pair in rubies and diamonds (see p. 60).

Shortly after Barbara's marriage to the Count, she travelled with him and her playboy cousin Jimmy Donahue to his family home in Denmark, Hardenberg Castle, to meet the rest of his family. Their arrival coincided with news of Alexis Mdivani's death in a car accident in Spain, which plunged Barbara into a state

Barbara photographed at the Everglades Club in Palm Beach in 1941. She is wearing pearl and diamond ear clips; pearls were her favourite gems.

A pair of natural black and white pearls mounted in a double border of pear-shaped diamonds, acquired by Barbara in the 1950s from Bulgari, Rome.

of depression during most of the visit. Her spirits were lifted by the dinner party that her brother-in-law Henrik hosted for neighbouring gentry and European diplomats. After the gathering he presented her with a bracelet set with the family emeralds. She was thrilled: 'It's the first time I've ever really been given a present I didn't have to pay for myself.' It has been suggested that Tiffany's, New York, made the bracelet but it is more likely that this is the jewel commissioned by Henrik from Cartier in London on 31 May 1935 and for which he supplied the emeralds (p. 147).

After Barbara divorced his brother in 1938, Henrik wrote a brusque letter requesting the return of the bracelet: 'The emeralds are family stones and since you are no longer in the family I think they should be returned.' Although she was shocked by his tone, it is likely she complied with his request, and the emerald and diamond bracelet auctioned in Geneva in 1971 with the provenance of the late Count Henrik Haugwitz-Hardenberg-Reventlow was probably that jewel.

While Barbara was still married to the count, she made one of her most famous acquisitions from Cartier: the Romanov emeralds, once in the possession of the Grand Duchess Vladimir of Russia. Early in the century, the emeralds had been bought by the Chicago tycoon

Harold McCormick for his first wife, who was John D. Rockefeller's daughter Edith. They had been mounted in the style fashionable in the 1920s, as a *sautoir*: a long necklace that would complement the straight lines of the new dress styles. After Edith's death in 1932 the stones were unmounted and sold by the executors of her will to Cartier for $480,000. It reportedly cost Barbara over one million dollars to acquire them and the related publicity did not assist the Woolworth management in their wage negotiations with the staff.

Initially, Barbara commissioned Cartier in London to create a ring, a pair of earrings and a necklace, with the largest emerald, weighing 100 cts, set at the centre of the necklace. In 1947, now the wife of Prince Troubetzkoy (after a brief wartime marriage to the actor Cary Grant), Barbara instructed Lucien Lachassagne at Cartier to design an Indian style necklace/tiara, mounted in yellow gold instead of the more fashionable platinum (p. 151). Barbara loved to wear this extraordinary creation with a pair of cabochon emerald and diamond pendent earrings and a sari while receiving guests at her luxurious palace, Sidi Hosni, next to the Kasbah in Tangier, Morocco (p. 140). In 1965, she sold the jewel to Van Cleef & Arpels, who subsequently decided, because of the enormous value

A pair of ear clips set with two Burmese rubies weighing together approximately 9 cts, surrounded by large brilliant-cut diamonds.

In the photograph Barbara is with her third husband, the actor Cary Grant, to whom she was married from 1942 to 1945. She is wearing some of her ruby and diamond jewelry, including two bangles of Indian inspiration.

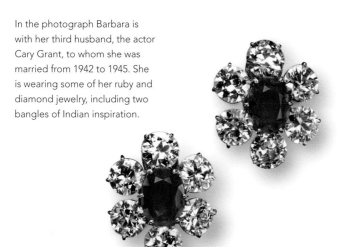

of the emeralds, to sell the stones individually. They remounted them into several jewels and had the largest hexagonal emerald re-cut to a cushion shape of 89.48 cts in order to remove flaws created by its previous unmountings. Van Cleef & Arpels wisely did not destroy the necklace itself and sold it in 1972 to the philanthropist Brooke Astor, a devoted client of the firm. In order to make the necklace the right size for Mrs Astor, four links were removed and cultured pearl pendants with yellow gold and diamond caps were suspended where the emeralds had been. A pair of yellow gold, diamond and cultured-pearl pendent earrings were made by the firm to match the necklace.

In 1967, Barbara instructed Van Cleef & Arpels to design a new head ornament for her. They created an extraordinary diadem, which had as a central motif a pear-shaped diamond of 54.82 cts. It was further decorated by three other diamonds of 29.49, 10.95 and 10.67 cts, as well as almost 80 cts of other diamonds. The light setting in platinum gave the impression that the stones were almost floating above her head.

It was from Bulgari that Barbara bought the famous 40 cts 'Pasha' diamond, believed to be of Indian origin, which, at the time that it was acquired by the Viceroy of Egypt, Ibrahim Pasha, in 1848, was said to be the finest stone in the Egyptian treasury. Its whereabouts were unknown for many years until Bulgari bought it from King Farouk of Egypt. Unhappy with its slightly octagonal form, Barbara had it re-cut at Cartier to a weight of 38.19 cts and mounted as a dazzling ring. When she died her 'resident manager', Bill Robertson, is said to have removed the ring from her finger and, somewhat bizarrely, placed it along with the contents of her three jewelry cases in a brown paper bag, which was taken to Bermuda, where her will was probated, to await the dispersal of her bequests.

Barbara was sometimes tempted away from Cartier and Van Cleef & Arpels by other fashionable jewelers, such as Fulco di Verdura. In the mid-1960s she acquired from him a pink topaz and diamond 'flower twist' *parure*, perhaps to complement the colour of a dress (p. 153). She surely could not have known that her fellow heiress, friend and rival, Doris Duke, possessed an almost identical *parure*. They not only had the same taste in jewelry, but also in men: they both married (albeit briefly) the Dominican diplomat Porfirio Rubirosa – Doris in 1947, Barbara in 1953.

Opposite
Barbara wearing the Vladimir emeralds as a tiara, together with a pair of emerald and diamond pendent earrings and the Marie Antoinette pearl necklace. The photograph was taken in 1961 by Cecil Beaton at Sidi Hosni, her palace in Tangier, where she held legendary parties.

In Paris in 1947, Lucien Lachassagne, one of Cartier's great designers, created the final version of an emerald and diamond necklace for Barbara using the Romanov emeralds. He remounted the seven largest emeralds in yellow gold as the fringe of a diamond necklace/tiara of Indian inspiration. In 1967, Barbara sold the necklace to Van Cleef & Arpels. They removed the seven emeralds and sold them separately. The necklace itself was later sold to the philanthropist and socialite Brooke Astor. In the photograph above, the area in colour indicates the necklace that still survives, with the position once held by the emeralds shown in black and white.

A two-row golden cultured pearl necklace with a black opal and diamond clasp by Cartier.

Opposite
A group of jewels from Barbara's collection, including moonstone and diamond ear clips and ring, a pink topaz and diamond 'flower twist' *parure* by Verdura, and one of her favourite black opals mounted as a brooch in a double cluster of brilliant-cut diamonds.

Barbara was attracted to unusual stones, such as harlequin opals. She liked their fantastic play of colours and used them in clasps for her pearl necklaces as well as for a matching brooch. She also loved the unusual adularescence of moonstones and the play of light on them. In the 1930s, she had a moonstone *parure* created by Van Cleef & Arpels; in 1998 a pair of ear clips and a matching ring with moonstones in a double cluster of diamonds appeared at auction in Geneva (p. 153).

In the postwar years the 'Great Cat' jewels, inspired by Cartier's director of fine jewelry, Jeanne Toussaint,

and created by the designer Peter Lemarchand, were very popular with the stylish women of the day, including Barbara. She chose three of the finest examples: a brooch, a pair of earrings and a bracelet, dated 1957, 1961 and 1962 respectively (p. 154). Designed as tigers, the brooch and the earrings echo the bold curve of the badge of the Order of the Golden Fleece, the 'pelts' set with onyx and fancy yellow diamond stripes.

Barbara was also known for her elegant homes. These included Winfield House, a neo-Georgian mansion that she had built in Regent's Park in London

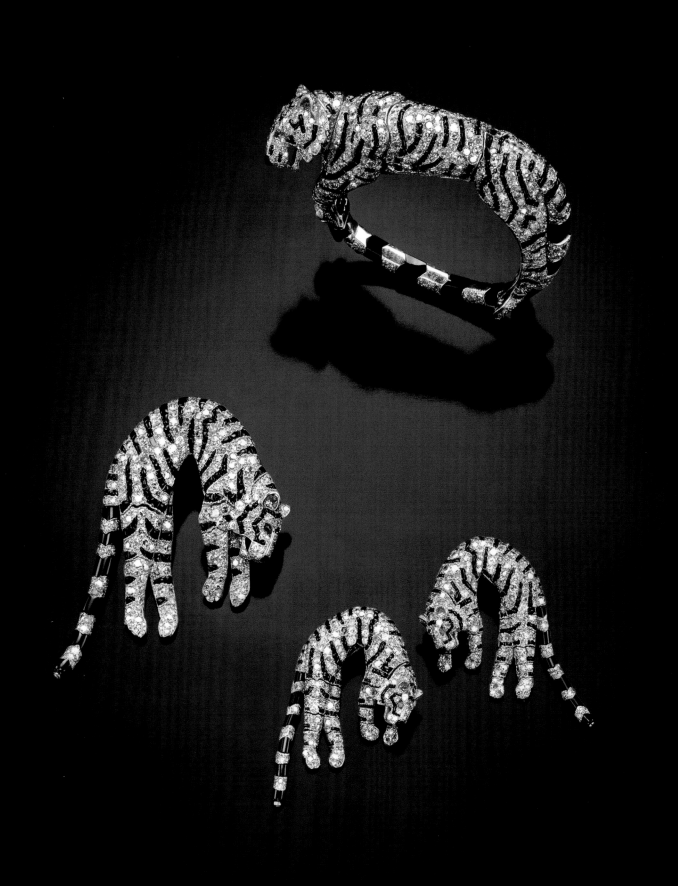

Barbara Hutton in the early 1960s, wearing the tiger brooch as well as her golden cultured pearl two-strand necklace.

Opposite
Barbara Hutton's fancy yellow diamond and onyx 'Great Cat' jewels by Cartier, Paris. The tiger brooch was made in 1957, the earrings in 1961 and the bracelet in 1962.

in the late 1930s after her son, Lance Reventlow, was born. The outbreak of war meant she barely used the property and in 1945 she offered it to the US government for one dollar. It is now the residence of the American Ambassador. After the war Barbara lavishly entertained friends from around the world at Sidi Hosni, her palace in Tangier, and built a Japanese-style villa called Sumiya in Cuernavaca, Mexico.

Barbara continued to look for happiness in marriage, but two further husbands were also divorced. After the death of Lance in a plane crash in 1972, she became totally isolated and spent her last years bedridden. She died of heart failure in her suite at the Beverly Wilshire Hotel in Los Angeles in May 1979, at the age of 66. Sadly, her way of life, *naïveté* and her

need for affection made her rely on people who took advantage of her and she was known for her generosity to virtual strangers. This is why most of her fortune had gone. She was buried in the Woolworth mausoleum at Woodlawn Cemetery in the Bronx, New York.

During her lifetime Barbara amassed a remarkable collection of jewelry. The few pieces that can be identified as belonging to her are a tribute to a lady with a great sense of beauty and style. Certainly, to Barbara her jewelry was not only a tangible expression of her great wealth but also a source of comfort. What she found in her gemstones was the combination of durability and perfection that she never obtained in her own troubled life. ✖

Merle Oberon

7

Merle Oberon had an unusual exotic beauty that, combined with grace and style, secured her a sparkling film career in Britain and Hollywood. She played opposite Leslie Howard in *The Scarlet Pimpernel* (1934) and was nominated for an Academy Award for her role in *The Dark Angel* (1935), but she is perhaps best known for her portrayal of Cathy Earnshaw in *Wuthering Heights* (1939), performing with Laurence Olivier and David Niven. Her success – she was reputedly paid $60,000 for playing Kitty Vane in *The Dark Angel* – enabled her to indulge her taste for exquisite jewels, which she both purchased and was given.

Merle's origins have always been shrouded in mystery; the actress was vague about her parentage and place of birth because her mother's dark skin was a cause of embarrassment in an era of racial prejudice. It seems she was born Estelle Merle O'Brien Thompson on 19 February 1911 in Bombay, at the height of the British Raj, and was the daughter of a Eurasian mother and an English father, who was a railway engineer. Patriotism led him to the battlefields of France in the First World War, where he died of pneumonia. Merle and her mother then moved to Calcutta, where the young girl won a scholarship to a prestigious school, but it was here that she began to experience the feeling of shame about her parentage that would remain with her all her life. In later years Merle claimed to come from Tasmania and that her mother was her maid.

By the late 1920s Merle's stunning looks meant she was never short of an eligible beau to partner her to the dance hall. She performed in amateur dramatics and developed a great passion for films just as 'talkies' arrived. So, when one of her admirers, Colonel Ben Finney, a former actor, offered her the chance to go to France and meet Rex Ingram, the famous film director,

she leapt at it. Finney's apparent generosity had an ulterior motive, however. He had by chance met her mother and he did not wish to be involved with someone of mixed race. The Colonel was leaving for France and he had no intention of meeting Merle should she in fact go there. Unaware of the intended betrayal, Merle and her mother sailed for Europe. Though there was no sign of Finney, she did contrive to meet Ingram, who gave her a role as an extra in *The Three Passions* (1929). In London, she found jobs as a club hostess in establishments such as the Café de Paris, frequented by the Prince of Wales and his circle, and graduated from an extra to playing small parts in films.

In 1931, Alexander Korda, who had started out as a film producer and director in his native Hungary and gone on to work in Berlin, Paris and Hollywood, arrived in England and set up his company London Films. He spotted Merle and not only gave her the cameo role of Anne Boleyn opposite Charles Laughton in *The Private Life of Henry VIII* (1933) but also the screen name with which she would become famous.

The success of that period film on both sides of the Atlantic gave the young actress an entrée to the elite of the film world. In 1934, Merle was briefly engaged to Joseph Schenck, co-founder of 20th Century Pictures, who is reputed to have showered her with jewels and the promise of Hollywood roles. When the engagement was broken off, she returned the expensive diamond ring he had given her. It was Korda who took her to Hollywood, where she starred with Maurice Chevalier in *Folies Bergère de Paris* (1935). The business-minded Korda sold part of her contract to Sam Goldwyn and for the rest of the decade she featured in films made in London and Hollywood.

This was also the period when she acquired one of her most treasured jewels, which she wore frequently,

both on and off the screen. The antique emerald and diamond necklace consists of festoons and clusters fringed by emerald and diamond drops in a style typical of the 1860s (p. 161). The central motif can also be detached and worn as a brooch. According to legend, the necklace had been presented by the Emperor Napoleon III to Baroness Haussmann, whose husband planned the redevelopment of Paris during the Second Empire. At some later date, two of the emerald and diamond drops had been converted into a pair of earrings. In *The Divorce of Lady X* (1938), in which she starred with Laurence Olivier, Merle wore the necklace to great effect.

The young actress worked and played hard and her name was often linked with prominent names in the film world, such as her co-stars Leslie Howard and David Niven. It became apparent, however, that the feelings she and Korda had for each other and the interests they shared went beyond their business contract. He was nearly twenty years older than the actress – and later complained that she treated him as a father figure – but nonetheless they were married in the town hall in Antibes on 3 June 1939. It was a small ceremony and the witnesses were an old friend, Henri Guenot of Juan-les-Pins, and Mme Suzanne Blum, a Paris lawyer who acted for Merle and later for the Duchess of Windsor.

Korda bought his new wife three superb diamond brooches from Cartier, London, as a wedding present. They had originally been part of a head ornament and were all in the form of a rose in full bloom, set with diamonds, the largest with the diamond pistils mounted *en tremblant.* Merle wore them as clips on her dress or attached to a ribbon around her neck and the effect was sensational. In the sale of her collection at Christie's in New York on 22 April 1980, the clips were unfortunately sold as two separate lots.

Interestingly, when HRH Princess Elizabeth married Lt Philip Mountbatten in 1947 she was given a similar set of diamond clips, mounted in a tiara by Cartier, by the Nizam of Hyderabad. In 1973, Her Majesty the Queen had the diamonds in the tiara unmounted to form a new tiara with Burmese rubies, but she kept the three clips, which she is still often seen wearing.

Two diamond clips made in 1939 were also sold separately at the auction of Merle's jewelry collection.

Merle Oberon photographed
by Horst in 1942 wearing three
flowerhead clips that were a
wedding present from Alexander
Korda in 1939. The clips (below)
by Cartier, London, had originally
formed part of a hair ornament.

Opposite
Two ruby and diamond
flowerhead clips by Cartier,
London, 1939, and three
photographs from the Cartier,
Paris, archives, showing how
the clips could also be
mounted as the centrepiece
of a diamond bracelet.

Page 156
Merle Oberon photographed in
the mid-1960s wearing her ruby
and diamond pendent ear clips.

A sapphire and diamond
five-petalled flower brooch
created by Cartier in 1940 with
a detachable diamond stem.

The clips, both designed as flowerheads with, respectively, diamond and ruby pistils, were designed to be worn together or separately, or could be attached to a diamond strap bracelet to form an impressive clasp, as shown in photographs from the Cartier, Paris, archives (p. 158). Merle wore this bracelet, as well as the three rose clips, in the film *'Til We Meet Again* (1940).

The same year that film was released, Merle acquired a superb sapphire and diamond floral brooch from Cartier, London (p. 156). The detachable flowerhead clip was set with a large oval sapphire centre and the petals were *pavé*-set with diamonds. At the 1980 auction, the diamond stem was sold separately, with no mention of the fact that it could be attached to the flowerhead clip. Merle wore the two together on many occasions but she also wore the flowerhead clip on a velvet band as the centre of a choker and on a platinum bangle that was also supplied by Cartier. Another pair of Cartier diamond flowerhead clips was designed with a detachable chain of baguette and fancy-cut diamonds. Simply by having the chain attached, the jewel became a stylish garment clasp. It is apparent that Merle not only loved Cartier jewels, but also their versatility.

From the same period, but unsigned, were a pair of diamond feather scroll clips (p. 167) and a pair of ruby, blue and yellow sapphire ornaments of flowerhead and foliate design. The latter are probably the clips that could also be used as the centre of a tubogas (gas pipe) gold chain necklace, which, in turn, could become a bracelet: a typical example of Van Cleef & Arpels's work during those years.

In November 1938, Korda bought an incomparable emerald bead and diamond necklace for Merle from Cartier in London. It was designed as a fringe of twenty-nine graduated emerald drops, capped by diamonds, on a collar of diamond-set rondels linked by a platinum chain (p. 165). Indian in inspiration, it matched Merle's exotic looks.

The couple made their home at Denham, next to Korda's film studios, but the outbreak of war in September 1939 complicated their lives. Merle, now under contract to Warner Brothers, returned to Hollywood, and in 1940 Korda moved there to finish filming *The Thief of Bagdad* (1940). Although his departure at a critical moment of the war attracted criticism, it is thought that he was in fact doing work for the British secret services and his connections in America

Merle and the gossip columnist Walter Winchell photographed at the Stork Club in New York in 1940. She is wearing the emerald and diamond necklace created for her by Cartier, London, in 1938. It was designed as a chain of flexible circular-cut diamond roundels supporting twenty-nine graduated tumble cabochon emeralds with diamond tips (opposite).

were considered an asset at a time when the government wished to win over US public opinion. Churchill, in particular, thought that films could play a key role in this endeavour, as indeed proved to be the case with Korda's next film, *That Hamilton Woman* (1941), which drew parallels between Napoleon and Hitler and was a huge success in Britain, America and the USSR. Korda was granted a knighthood in recognition of his services to his adopted country and on 22 September 1942 Merle accompanied her husband to Buckingham Palace for his investiture by King George VI.

Unfortunately, Korda's work often left Merle alone and the marriage became strained. She busied herself with helping the British war effort and pursuing her career, appearing in historical dramas such as *The Lodger* (1944) and *A Song to Remember* (1945). After the couple divorced in 1945, Merle married Lucien Ballard, a successful Hollywood cameraman. By the time this relationship, too, had ended in divorce in 1949, Merle was deeply committed to Count Giorgio Cini. Their whirlwind romance is said to have resulted in several gifts of jewelry. Tragically, that same year,

the Count, while he was still trying to persuade his disapproving parents to accept Merle as his bride, was killed in a plane crash. Merle was devastated and threw herself back into film work.

In 1956, her life took a new turn when she became involved with Bruno Pagliai, a powerful and extremely wealthy cosmopolitan businessman in Mexico, and a year later they were married in Rome. The couple lived in Cuernavaca, some fifty miles south of Mexico City, where Barbara Hutton also had a property, and they adopted two Italian children, Bruno and Francesca. Merle's film appearances were rare from then on and she devoted herself to a full and glittering round of social events, friendships with princes and presidents, and indulged her appetite for fine clothes and jewelry.

In the late 1950s and 1960s Merle acquired many new jewels, which were complemented by dresses designed by Luis Estévez. 'Without security it is difficult for a woman to look or feel beautiful', she once remarked and Pagliai provided her with luxury and security. Some of her beautiful jewelry came from the Roman firm of Bulgari, such as a ruby and diamond

Merle at the Polo Ball in Palm Beach, Florida, in 1955. The ruby and diamond ear clips that she is wearing were later mounted as pendants, and the ruby and diamond necklace was subsequently redesigned by David Webb.

Below
The pair of ruby and diamond pendants, weighing respectively 13.22 and 13.75 cts, in a cluster of twelve graduated, circular-cut diamonds, and a lozenge-cut ruby weighing approximately 12.13 cts mounted as a ring in a cluster of circular-cut diamonds with *pavé*-set diamond shoulders, created for Merle by David Webb.

Merle at the Polo Ball, Palm Beach, 1955. Behind her are the Duke of Windsor and the socialite Mrs C. Z. Guest.

Below
A pair of stylized feather brooches from the 1930s and a barrette brooch by Bulgari. The brooch is set with a step-cut diamond weighing approximately 15.30 cts, two trapeze-cut diamonds weighing approximately 3.34 and 3.37 cts, and two triangular-cut diamonds.

brooch designed as a bouquet with the flowers mounted *en tremblant* (p. 173). Bulgari was renowned for these stylish brooches in the late 1950s. A stunning diamond brooch was also supplied by Bulgari in this period. It has a lozenge outline and is set with a step-cut diamond weighing 15.30 cts at the centre, two trapeze-cut diamonds weighing approximately 3.34 and 3.37 cts, and two triangular-cut diamonds (right).

Merle altered many of her pieces at this time. The diamond clasp of the two-row emerald bead necklace (p. 165) was originally the clasp of a pearl and diamond bracelet. She was obviously extremely fond of emeralds: to match the necklace she acquired a pair of emerald and diamond ear clips from the American jewelry designer David Webb and a cabochon emerald and diamond ring from Harry Winston. One of the finest emeralds in her collection was a step-cut stone, mounted as a brooch, at the centre of a foliate diamond border, unsigned but probably by Van Cleef & Arpels.

Pearls were still fashionable and Merle had a pair of natural pearl earrings that were surmounted by circular-cut diamonds; she wore these with a single-row cultured pearl necklace. The stylish *bombé* diamond cluster clasp of the necklace was originally a ring.

A coral and diamond necklace
and pendent earrings by Van
Cleef & Arpels. The necklace
pendant could also be worn
as a brooch.

Merle in Acapulco, Mexico, dancing with former Mexican president Don Miguel Alemán in 1966. She is wearing the turquoise and diamond four-leafed clover ear clips illustrated below. The clips and the matching brooch were probably made by Bulgari. The turquoise and diamond bracelet was by Donadio, Naples.

Merle liked to spend time in Italy, especially Rome, where she enjoyed visiting the fashionable shops on the via Condotti. At Bulgari she bought an evening bag that she used on many occasions. It had an unusual design of stylized acorns and a gold clasp set with turquoise and diamonds.

In 1966, Merle played a glamorous duchess who wore fabulous jewels in the film version of Arthur Hailey's popular novel *Hotel*. The director, aware of the star's own wonderful collection, persuaded her to wear some of her jewelry in the production. Both in the film and the publicity portraits she wore a turquoise and diamond *parure*. The necklace was designed as a fringe of oval turquoise and diamond clusters with a large pear-shaped turquoise drop at the centre. The pendent earrings were of similar design.

The turquoise and diamond necklace, brooch and earrings that were included in the 1980 sale were almost certainly a reworking of a *parure* by Van Cleef & Arpels from the early 1970s. Her collection also contained a quatrefoil brooch and matching earrings, probably by Bulgari, and a bracelet, all set with turquoise and diamonds and dating from about the same era (p. 169). Van Cleef & Arpels also created her pink coral and diamond necklace, which could be converted into a choker and bracelet. The large pear-shaped cluster pendant could be worn as a brooch (p. 168).

Merle also owned several important ruby and diamond jewels, including a five-row ruby bead necklace and a ruby and diamond necklace from the 1950s (p. 166) that David Webb remounted for her in the 1960s.

Opposite
Merle (far left) at the Ballo Romantico held in the St Regis Hotel, New York, in December 1965. She is with Charlotte and Anne, the daughters of Henry Ford II, and the industrialist's second wife, Cristina. In Merle's hair is the diamond cluster necklace set with pear-shaped and brilliant-cut diamonds (above). The pear-shaped diamond weighing 17.99 cts, of D colour, was originally set in a ring.

Merle (seated right, next to the Duke of Windsor) photographed by
Raymond Depardon at the My Fair Lady Ball hosted by Hélène Rochas
in Paris, 1965. She is wearing ruby and diamond jewels, including a ruby
and diamond bouquet by Bulgari with the flowers mounted *en tremblant*
(right). On her head she wears the ruby and diamond necklace (opposite)
created by David Webb in the 1960s. The design of *entrelac de rubans*
has cabochon and oval-cut rubies intertwined with baguette and circular-
cut diamonds and a cushion-shaped ruby and baguette diamond tassel.
It was inspired by the ruby and diamond necklace made by Van Cleef &
Arpels in 1939 for the Duchess of Windsor (seated left) and worn by her
to the ball.

Opposite
Merle at a gala ball at the Plaza Hotel in New York in November 1970. A ring set with her pear-shaped diamond can be seen on her left hand. She is also wearing the pair of diamond chandelier earrings illustrated at right. The eight largest pear-shaped diamonds in these earrings weigh approximately 31 cts, and the six largest circular-cut diamonds weigh approximately 15 cts. The diamond cascade could be detached from the top element, which could then be used to support the ruby and diamond cluster pendant (p. 166), a pair of cabochon emerald drops, a pair of drop pearls, or the largest pear-shaped diamond from the central line of the cascade. The photograph also shows Merle wearing the diamond bracelet illustrated below in her hair. It was designed as a line of nine pear- and cushion-shaped diamonds, the largest weighing 7.75 cts. The total weight is over 41 cts.

The new setting was reminiscent in style of the necklace created by Van Cleef & Arpels for the Duchess of Windsor in 1939 (see pp. 172–173). David Webb also created Merle's ruby and diamond ring, set at the centre with a lozenge-shaped ruby weighing approximately 12 cts. She also had a pair of ruby and diamond pendants, each centred by an oval ruby of over 13 cts in a cluster of brilliant-cut diamonds, which she could hang from diamond surmounts as earrings (pp. 156 and 166).

These surmounts could also be used to support other drops, including two important cabochon emeralds, weighing together over 70 cts, with diamond caps and drop-shaped cultured pearls capped by marquise-shaped diamonds. By far the most important drops, however, were the ones designed as cascades of pear-shaped and brilliant-cut diamonds (above); the largest pear-shaped stone could be detached and worn singly as a drop. The actress would often wear these with her sensational diamond necklace of flowerhead cluster design set with diamonds of similar shape to the earrings (p. 171). On occasion, she wore this as a head ornament entwined in her coiffure, such as at the Ballo Romantico in New York in 1965 (p. 170) and at the opening of the film *Hotel*. Merle also owned a diamond bracelet of classical design that she could wear to decorate her hair. The single row of pear- and cushion-shaped diamonds weighed over 41 cts (above).

In 1973, the year she divorced Bruno Pagliai, Merle made her last film, *Interval*, in which the Dutch actor Robert Wolders played a young man who falls in love with an ageing star. Two years later, life imitated art when Merle married Wolders, twenty-five years her junior. They lived happily in Malibu until her death from a stroke in 1979.

The thirty-eight pieces of her jewelry sold in the 1980 sale not only represented Merle's stylish way of life and memorable moments in her career, but also the work of some of the finest jewelers of her era. ✠

The Maharani
Sita Devi of Baroda

---8---

When one considers the splendid jewels belonging to the Maharani Sita Devi of Baroda, the words that spring to mind are 'magical' and 'outstanding'. They were mostly the creation of Van Cleef & Arpels, and the combination of the skills of the eminent jeweler, the client's loyal devotion and, most importantly, the marvellous stones from the Baroda treasury, led to some of the most striking jewels produced in the period from the mid-1940s to the 1960s.

Sita Devi was born in Madras on 12 May 1917, the daughter of the Zamindar of Pithapuram, a wealthy landowner. Her first marriage was to the Zamindar of Vayyur, with whom she had three children. In 1943, when she was still only 26, she met Pratap Singh Rao Gaekwar of Baroda at the Madras horse races. He was the Maharaja of a princely state (now part of Gujarat) in western India that was one of the most senior in precedence – indicated by the firing of a 21-gun salute for the ruler – as well as one of the wealthiest because of a flourishing cotton industry. The Maharaja was considered to be among the richest men in the world.

It was love at first sight, but there were many obstacles to the couple's union. In addition to the fact that Sita Devi was married, the 35-year-old Maharaja had a wife and eight children. Once the relationship became known, it caused a scandal at the highest levels of society, both in India and in Britain, which was still the ruling power on the subcontinent.

The Maharaja's lawyers suggested that as a way out of her marriage Sita Devi could renounce her Hindu religion and convert to Islam and ask her husband to do the same. This she did and, as expected, the Zamindar refused to convert and so Sita Devi divorced him under Islamic law, which does not permit a woman of the Muslim faith to take a non-Muslim husband. This

sleight of hand freed Sita Devi from her first marriage; she then reverted to Hinduism and married the Maharaja of Baroda.

On his side, matters were also complicated. Viscount Wavell, the Viceroy of India, informed Pratap Singh Rao that he had broken the law against bigamy introduced by his grandfather Sayaji Rao Gaekwar. This enlightened ruler, whom Pratap Singh Rao succeeded as Maharaja in 1939, had declared that no man in Baroda could marry for a second time if his first wife was still alive and was not divorced from him. Sayaji Rao Gaekwar himself had been married for over fifty years and employed European tutors to educate his wife and introduce her to the progressive ideas that he believed in. She became a well-known campaigner for women's rights and was the president of the first All-India Women's Conference on Educational Reform in 1927. Sayaji Rao Gaekwar lifted Baroda out of the Middle Ages, was a patron of the arts and education, and founded the Bank of Baroda, today the third largest bank in India.

Pratap Singh Rao was not such a distinguished ruler as his grandfather and later he was deposed and exiled. In response to the accusation that his marriage to Sita Devi broke the law, he claimed that the Maharaja was exempt from such rules and that they applied only to the populace. He won the argument but the British government refused to acknowledge Sita Devi as 'Her Highness' and the press soon nicknamed her 'the Wallis Simpson of India'.

In March 1945, Sita Devi gave birth to the couple's only child, Maharajkumar Sayaji Rao Gaekwar, known as 'Princie'. Once the Second World War was over and international travel became possible, the family decided to seek a home in Europe and put all the fuss over the marriage behind them. They found the perfect location

Page 176
The Maharani Sita Devi of Baroda in Epsom, Surrey, 1946.

A detail of the emerald and diamond Van Cleef & Arpels necklace, 1950 (p. 187).

Sita Devi fastening the famous Baroda pearls around the neck of her husband, Maharaja Pratap Singh Gaekwar of Baroda, for the celebration of his fortieth birthday in 1948. The photograph is by Henri Cartier-Bresson.

Opposite
A necklace formed of two strings of the Baroda pearls. The pearls measure from 9.47 to 16.04 mm and the clasp is set with an old-mine-cut diamond weighing almost 9 cts in a cluster of diamonds.

in Monaco, where Sita Devi took up permanent residence. The Maharaja brought some of the most precious objects from the Baroda treasury to Monte Carlo and later passed official ownership of the jewels to the Maharani. Meanwhile, in New York in 1946, Sita Devi acquired a gold *minaudière* from Van Cleef & Arpels that was set with rubies, sapphires, emeralds and diamonds; the image was of the Empress Eugénie surrounded by her ladies-in-waiting, taken from a Winterhalter painting of 1855 (p. 182).

In India, the postwar years brought turmoil and transition. The country gained its independence in August 1947 and this heralded a change to the status of the princely states. The following year, in a last show of the old order before Baroda formally acceded to the Union of India, the state celebrated the fortieth birthday of the ruler. The festivities were particularly lavish, accompanied by great pomp and circumstance. A week's holiday was declared and there was a variety of entertainments, including an elephant parade and musical

Sita Devi and her son 'Princie' (wearing one of her necklaces) preparing for the Maharaja's fortieth birthday celebrations in 1948, photographed by Henri Cartier-Bresson. She is wearing the Baroda diamond necklace, set at the centre with the 'Star of the South' diamond of 128 cts and the pear-shaped 'English Dresden' diamond of 78 cts. On her left hand the Maharani is wearing a pearl ring that was later remounted by Van Cleef & Arpels as the clasp of a pearl bracelet.

In the photograph above Sita Devi is wearing a bracelet similar to the President Vargas diamond bracelet by Harry Winston, which is set with 7 step-cut diamonds ranging from 18 to 31 cts, all faceted from the same rough diamond discovered in 1938 in the San Antônio river, Minas Gerais, Brazil.

shows. For the occasion, the Maharaja wore the famous seven-strand Baroda pearl necklace, which had been created for one of his predecessors, a noted jewelry collector, in the mid-19th century.

At the celebrations the beautiful Sita Devi was glittering with an enormous three-strand diamond necklace set at the centre with the 'Star of the South', a cushion-shaped diamond of 128 cts, and, underneath, the 'English Dresden', a pear-shaped diamond of 78 cts. The other jewels that she wore included a button-shaped pearl ring and a diamond bracelet very similar to one created by Harry Winston in 1947 from a 726.60 cts rough diamond found in Minas Gerais and named in honour of the Brazilian president Getúlio Vargas.

180

The Maharaja of Baroda
enthroned at Laxmi Villas Palace
in Baroda at the beginning of the
Durbar to celebrate his fortieth
birthday in 1948. He is wearing the
Baroda pearls.

An emerald and diamond *sarpech*
(turban ornament) mounted in
platinum and set with circular-
cut and baguette diamonds. In
the centre is a cushion-shaped
cabochon emerald, engraved
with a lotus flower, of 38.95 cts.
A pear-shaped cabochon emerald
is suspended from the scroll
surmount.

A studio portrait of Sita Devi, taken in December 1944 by Paul Popper. She is wearing her favourite pearl jewels.

A gold and gem-set *minaudière* from Van Cleef & Arpels, 1946. The design on the lid, set in rubies, sapphires, emeralds and diamonds, was based on a painting of the Empress Eugénie surrounded by her ladies-in-waiting by Franz Xaver Winterhalter, 1855.

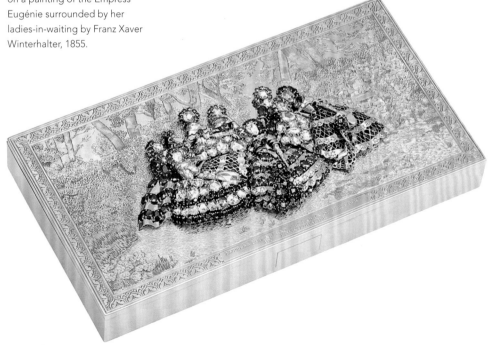

Opposite
An antique Indian necklace set with ruby and emerald beads and pearls, with a central plaque of table diamonds. The gold fastening was added in the late 1940s.

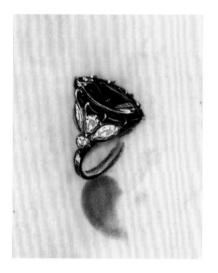

Designs of jewels created for Sita Devi by Van Cleef & Arpels. Clockwise, from top left: An emerald and diamond brooch, c. 1950; a diamond brooch set with a cabochon emerald engraved with flowers inlaid with gold and rubies, c. 1946; a ring with a marquise-shaped sapphire of 34.77 cts and navette diamond shoulders, 1954; a ring with an oval ruby of 8.37 cts that was recut to 7.95 cts, 1950.

When she stayed at the George V hotel in Paris on her trip to Europe in 1946, Sita Devi paid her first visit to Van Cleef & Arpels in the Place Véndome. It was the beginning of the love story between the Maharani and the firm, which resulted in some of the most beautiful jewelry of the postwar era. On that – and subsequent – occasions she brought a bag full of jewels that she wanted to be remounted in modern settings. She did not wish to use her real name or title, preferring to be called 'Mrs Brown', to avoid publicity. The initial outcome of the visit was a pair of pendent earrings made with black and white pear-shaped pearls and diamonds. Two years later they were remodelled by Van Cleef & Arpels and consigned to her in January 1949; the earrings became one of the Maharani's most cherished pieces of jewelry (p. 185). The new design, with the pearls hanging from a flower set in diamonds, become a characteristic motif of Van Cleef & Arpels. In December 1948, the firm delivered a brooch in a 'constellation' design of platinum and diamonds from stones supplied by Sita Devi.

In 1949, Baroda formally acceded to India and the following year the Dominion of India became a republic. Once the government began to look into the finances

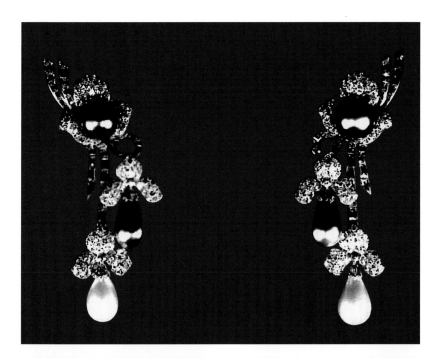

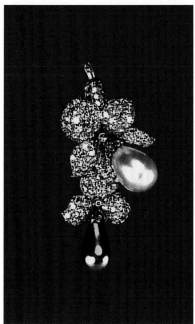

Below
Sita Devi at a reception in Trouville in 1960. She is wearing the Van Cleef & Arpels black and white pendent ear clips, her three-string pearl necklace and her black pearl and diamond bracelet by Cartier. The Maharani enjoyed smoking and used to say, 'a cigarette is just a cigarette, but a cigar is always a smoke'.

Top
Pendent ear clips of black and white pearls ordered by Sita Devi from Van Cleef & Arpels in October 1946; delivered 1947.

Above
The ear clips as remodelled by Van Cleef & Arpels and consigned to Sita Devi in January 1949.

The design of the emerald and diamond necklace ordered from Van Cleef & Arpels by Sita Devi in 1950. The necklace (opposite) was made of platinum, set with 1,260 brilliant-cut diamonds of 75.13 cts, 50 baguette diamonds of 4.48 cts, and cabochon emeralds, including 13 drops of 422 cts, all from Colombian mines.

of the former princely state, officials were shocked to discover not only the amount of money the Maharaja had taken but also that the treasury had been stripped of most of its valuable jewels and objects. These included the historic diamonds, the Baroda pearls, the famous Pearl Carpet, described by George F. Kunz and Charles H. Stevenson in 1908 as 'probably the most costly pearl ornament in the world', and a matching Pearl Canopy.

Under duress, the Maharaja repaid the money and returned the Baroda pearl necklace, although without several of the pearls, and the three-strand diamond necklace, but many of the state's most valuable pieces were never recovered. Sita Devi had had them reset, making them difficult to trace. In 1950, 'Mrs Brown' arranged for a number of items to be remounted by Van Cleef & Arpels. In March, she gave the firm several pear-shaped cabochon emeralds and diamonds set in

different jewels. The emeralds, with their homogenous and saturated colour, were a fine example of the quality of the gem stones that came from the Baroda treasury. The great French firm reworked them into a necklace in an Indian-inspired style (p. 187). The accompanying pendent earrings were of creole design with step-cut emeralds and baguette diamonds supporting a fringe of cabochon pear-shaped emeralds, with a diamond briolette hanging in the middle (p. 189).

In June 1950, 'Mrs Brown' asked if Van Cleef & Arpels could mount, '*le plus vite possible*' (as quickly as possible), a navette diamond of 13.10 cts as a ring. She also wanted a hexagonal emerald inset with a cushion-shaped diamond to be made into the centrepiece of a clasp for a pearl bracelet (p. 188). At the same time, she ordered a diamond bracelet set at the centre with a line of nine cushion-shaped diamonds ranging from

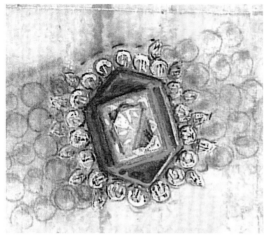

4 to 23 cts that belonged to her. The next month, she took in four pear-shaped diamonds of 15.16, 13.47, 12.26 and 12.10 cts, together with other diamonds, which were made into the wings of a butterfly brooch.

In April 1951, Nehru, the prime minister of India, announced that the Maharaja had been deposed for 'defying the authority of the Indian government'. He was given a month in which to appeal to the president, Rajendra Prasad, against his dismissal, while Sita Devi waited anxiously in London. His appeal failed and he was succeeded as titular ruler of Baroda by his 21-year-old son from his first marriage, Fateh Singh Rao Gaekwar. Not only did the Maharaja lose his title, but also the annual allowance of £200,000 from the privy purse. Nonetheless, his personal fortune was enormous and he was said to be the second richest man in India.

Despite being deposed, the Maharaja and his wife continued to use their titles and the crest of Baroda,

and the family maintained their luxurious lifestyle of the old days, residing in Monte Carlo and Paris and mixing in high society. The Maharaja indulged his passion for breeding and racing horses while Sita Devi, always swathed in the most beautiful embroidered saris and dripping with jewels, was a familiar sight at the most exclusive events.

In their style and settings, Sita Devi's gems conveyed something of the mystery and magic of India. When she was busy ordering jewels from Van Cleef & Arpels in 1950, 'Mrs Brown' requested a new setting for a Burmese oval ruby of 8.37 cts. The stone was recut to a new weight of 7.95 cts, set in a cluster of half-moon diamonds and decorated on the side with a motif of navette and brilliant-cut diamonds (p. 184).

Her taste for ruby and diamond jewelry was maintained through the 1950s. On 18 September 1952 she ordered a ring to be made with another extraordinary

A pair of emerald and diamond creole earrings by Van Cleef & Arpels, created in 1950 to accompany the emerald and diamond necklace (p. 187). They are set with ten octagonal-cut emeralds of 30 cts, ten emerald drops of 100 cts and two briolette diamonds of 38 cts.

A bracelet of emerald beads interspersed with brilliant-cut and baguette diamonds.

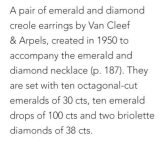

Opposite
The necklace (left) was created around 1860 for the Maharaja Khande Rao Gaekwar of Baroda. It was composed of five rows of large table-cut diamonds with a fringe of beads and pear-shaped cabochon emeralds. From this a pendant was suspended set with a hexagonal-shaped emerald inset with a cushion-shaped diamond and further decorated with briolette and table-cut diamonds and four large pear-shaped emeralds. Sita Devi had the necklace dismantled

in order to create new jewels. The hexagonal-shaped emerald inset with a cushion-shaped diamond in a border of brilliant-cut diamonds (illustrated) was used to form the centrepiece of a diamond clasp to a pearl bracelet that was created by Van Cleef & Arpels for Sita Devi in 1950 (drawing illustrated). According to the firm's Paris archives, the emerald weighed about 30 cts and the cushion-shaped diamond weighed approximately 12 cts.

A ruby, emerald and diamond
necklace created by Van Cleef &
Arpels for Sita Devi in 1954. The
gems were from her collection.

Opposite
Sita Devi with, from left, Princess
Grace of Monaco, Aristotle
Onassis, Maria Callas and Prince
Rainier of Monaco. Majorca,
July 1961.

ruby, an oval-shaped stone of 25.63 cts from the Mogok
mines in Burma. This gem, with its rich colour, known
as 'pigeon blood red', was set in platinum with brilliant-
cut and navette diamonds on the shoulders. In the same
month, she took seven faceted oval-shaped rubies, with
a total weight of 33 cts, and nine diamond briolettes,
with a total weight of 80 cts, all set in a necklace,
together with some loose diamonds, to Van Cleef &
Arpels. The firm created a classical new necklace with
a delicate platinum prong setting. The seven rubies
formed the central motif, supporting a fringe of diamond
briolettes (p. 193). The company made a pair of matching pendent ear clips, set at the centre with an
oval-shaped ruby in a border of baguette and brilliant-
cut diamonds supporting a fringe of diamond briolettes.
The quality of the stones and the elegance of the design,
together with the almost invisible setting, made the
set a superlative example of the platinum jewelry of
the 1950s.

In 1955, Van Cleef & Arpels created the 'Flamme'
ring setting in platinum and brilliant-cut diamonds for
another magnificent Burmese ruby of 12.33 cts that
belonged to Sita Devi. On 3 September 1960 she was
photographed resplendent in her ruby and diamond
jewelry at the famous 'royal ball' in Naples, hosted by

Duke Francesco and Duchess Elena Serra di Cassano
in the Palazzo Pizzofalcone to mark the opening of the
Olympic regatta. Sita Devi was accompanied by the
Baron Alexis de Redé and among the thousand illustrious guests her rubies were perhaps rivalled only by
those worn by Queen Frederica of Greece.

Sapphires were also much favoured by Sita Devi.
In May 1954, she took a beautiful marquise-shaped
sapphire of 34.77 cts to Van Cleef & Arpels. The firm
mounted it simply in a ring in a platinum prong setting,
with navette and brilliant-cut diamonds on the shoulders (p. 184). In July the same year, the firm created
an Indian-inspired set with stones whose unusual cut
indicated that they came from old Indian jewels. The
necklace of bib design was set in yellow gold and
encrusted with partly faceted cabochon rubies and
emeralds, interspersed with diamond-set leaf motifs
(p. 190). There was also a bracelet of matching design.

Sita Devi admired the elegant platinum prong
settings of the 1950s and had a diamond necklace made
with fifteen navette diamonds, with a total weight of
64.13 cts, mounted with baguette carrés and brilliant-
cut diamonds. She also ordered a 'palme' clip brooch
in baguette diamonds, with thirteen navette diamonds
that weighed a total of 22 cts (p. 194).

Two ruby and diamond bangles
set with a line of alternating
step-cut diamonds and rubies.
Sita Devi's collection contained
a similar pair of bangles set with
step-cut sapphires and rubies.

The 'royal ball' at the Palazzo
Pizzofalcone in Naples,
3 September 1960. From left
to right, Aristotle Onassis, the
Duchess Elena Serra di Cassano
(the hostess), an unidentified
gentleman, Sita Devi wearing
her ruby and diamond jewels,
and the Maharaja of Jaipur.

Opposite
The ruby and diamond necklace
created for Sita Devi by Van
Cleef & Arpels in 1954 using her
own stones. It was set with seven
oval-shaped rubies weighing
over 40 cts and nine briolette
diamonds weighing 115 cts.

The original design (top) and the completed pair (centre) of *crêtes de coq* (cockscomb) black pearl and diamond ear clips, created for Sita Devi in 1958, and (above) a 'palme' diamond clip brooch created in 1955, both by Van Cleef & Arpels.

Sita Devi with her son at Van Cleef & Arpels in 1960 admiring the 'Princie' diamond that was named after him. She is wearing her favourite pearl jewels, including the black pearl and diamond bracelet by Cartier, London, shown at right.

Design and photograph (top and centre) of the emerald and diamond clasp of a pearl bracelet created by Van Cleef & Arpels for Sita Devi in 1957. Above, the step-cut emerald of 43.70 cts in a cluster of brilliant-cut diamonds as it appeared in a Geneva auction on 12 May 1988.

In the years of exile the interests of the former Maharaja and his wife began to diverge and in 1956 the couple divorced. Pratap Singh Rao took up residence in London, where he died in 1968. After the divorce, Sita Devi continued to use the title of Maharani, and her Rolls-Royce in Monaco bore the Baroda coat of arms, although she was now even less entitled to do this. She kept up her luxurious lifestyle and travelled with her son all over the world attending society events. She maintained her jewelry collection and still commissioned pieces from Van Cleef & Arpels, as well as other jewelers. For example, in 1957 she had a step-cut 43.70 cts emerald mounted in a cluster of diamonds as the clasp of her pearl bracelet (left).

In 1958, Sita Devi had a new diamond clasp created for her sensational three-string pearl necklace (p. 196), using the 15.56 cts oval-shaped diamond that was originally set in the centre of a ruby and diamond clasp made for her by Van Cleef & Arpels in 1950. Now it was mounted in an *entrelac de rubans* design, set in diamonds (p. 197). The same year she had mounted two button pearls and two drop-shaped pearls as pendent earrings in a *genre ancien* (p. 198). Her two circular black pearls were mounted in platinum and brilliant-cut diamonds in a *crêtes de coq* (cockscomb) design (p. 194). Her extraordinary button-shaped natural pearl had an exceptionally beautiful pinkish-white colour and lustre, and with a weight of over 50 cts was considered one of the largest button pearls ever known. It was mounted in a ring that was part of the array of jewels the Maharani wore for her husband's fortieth birthday celebration in 1948 (p. 180), and ten years later the pearl became the centre of a clasp, designed as a flower and set with brilliant-cut diamonds, for a pearl bracelet (p. 198).

Sita Devi and Princie were the guests of honour at Van Cleef & Arpels in Paris in 1960 to celebrate the company's acquisition of a cushion-shaped pink diamond of 34.64 cts at auction at Sotheby's in London on 17 March. The diamond, from the Golconda mines in India, was rumoured to have stemmed from the collection of the Nizam of Hyderabad. At the reception the stone was named after the Maharani's son and since then has been known as the 'Princie' diamond.

By the mid-1960s the former Maharani's lavish lifestyle began to put her finances under strain and she secretly began to sell some of her stones and jewelry.

Before her divorce, she had occasionally sold pieces that she no longer wanted or that she wished to exchange for more up-to-date jewels. The emerald and diamond anklets that Harry Winston purchased from her in 1953 probably fell into this category. In 1957, the Duchess of Windsor was surprised, and not very pleased, to discover that one of her necklaces was made from these stones (see p. 85).

On 10 September 1965, Sita Devi sold a diamond ring accompanied by a note written on headed paper with the Baroda crest, and signed by her, that stated she was the sole owner of the pear-shaped diamond weighing 17.98 cts (p. 201). Despite her increasingly precarious pecuniary situation, the former Maharani continued to live in the grand style with Princie, who was now her main companion. They were charming and vivacious and appeared in *Esquire* magazine's list of 'fun couples' in 1969. But in the early 1970s, Sita Devi suffered further financial problems.

In 1971, Christie's in Geneva auctioned the antique hexagonal-shaped emerald inset with a cushion-shaped diamond that was the centrepiece of a diamond clasp.

Opposite
The Baroda pearl three-string
necklace. The clasp created by
Van Cleef & Arpels in 1958 with
an oval-shaped diamond (see
below) has been replaced by a
motif set with oval- and pear-
shaped diamonds.

Right
Sita Devi at the Hamburg Derby
– the German equivalent of the
Epsom Derby – in July 1959. She
is wearing her favourite pearl
necklace.

Below
The diamond clasp, and its
original design, created by Van
Cleef & Arpels in 1958 for Sita
Devi's pearl necklace. It was set
at the centre with a 15.56 cts
oval-shaped diamond.

Designs for a pair of pendent ear clips and a pearl bracelet, both by Van Cleef & Arpels, 1958. The ear clips, in a *genre ancien*, are each set with a button pearl and a drop-shaped pearl supplied by Sita Devi. The floral diamond clasp of the pearl bracelet is set at the centre with a button pearl that originally formed one her rings (p. 180).

Opposite
Sita Devi wearing her pearl pendent earrings and her pearl necklace in 1966.

Opposite
Sita Devi with her son Princie
at Paris's Vagenende restaurant
in June 1966. On her arm is the
Van Cleef & Arpels gem-set
minaudière from 1946 (p. 182).

Left
A ring set with a pear-shaped
diamond weighing 17.98 cts and
a note written in 1965 by Sita
Devi confirming her ownership
of the ring.

Below
A ring set with a step-cut
diamond weighing 35.07 cts.

This was the piece that 'Mrs Brown' had taken to Van Cleef & Arpels in 1950 and the clasp was for a pearl bracelet (p. 188). The catalogue noted that the emerald weighed about 30 cts and the inset diamond weighed approximately 12 cts and had originally been mounted in a ring. At the time of the sale, the emerald was still set with the clustered diamonds of the original clasp. The lot was accompanied by a letter signed by Sita Devi stating that according to family tradition the antique jewel was originally part of an aigrette. In reality, it formed part of the pendant of a diamond, cabochon emerald and bead necklace that had been created around 1860 for the Maharaja Khande Rao Gaekwar of Baroda (p. 188).

Sita Devi's finances were further affected by her decision to use her jewelry as a guarantee with the bank, because she did not realize that this would entail a heavy annual interest payment. Finally, on 16 November 1974, at the Crédit Mobilier de Monaco, the jewels that had been such an integral part of her life in high society were sold. The provenance was not mentioned in the catalogue, but such outstanding pieces were instantly recognizable. The sale included her cherished ruby collection, with its two ruby and diamond bangles (p. 192) and the spectacular 25.63 cts ruby, sold without its setting. Her three-string pearl necklace also went, although the 15 cts oval diamond that had formed its clasp was probably sold privately, as it had been replaced by a smaller stone in a border of pear-shaped diamonds (p. 196). An elegant black pearl and diamond bracelet by Cartier (p. 194) was one of the pieces that Sita Devi used to wear with her favourite black and white pearl pendent ear clips (p. 185). Both pieces were included, along with her other pearl jewels and her emerald *parure*. Her magnificent diamond ring (below), set with a cut-cornered rectangular step-cut diamond weighing 35.07 cts that originally came from the Golconda mines in India, was also sold, along with several antique Indian jewels.

The loss of her jewelry was not the only misfortune that befell the former Maharani in her later years and she faded out of the glittering world in which she had once sparkled. The premature death of Princie in

suspicious circumstances in 1985, at the age of only 40, left Sita Devi devastated. She never recovered and died on 15 February 1989 in Paris.

Since the sale of her jewelry in 1974, some of the Maharani's pieces have reappeared from time to time in international auctions where their exotic provenance always creates a stir. On 25 April 2007 a magnificent natural pearl necklace appeared at auction at Christie's in New York under the title 'The Baroda Pearls: Property of a Royal Family', although it is not known if the necklace ever belonged to Sita Devi herself. The two-strand necklace with pearls graduating from just under 10 mm to a little over 16 mm was of a quality befitting its illustrious origin.

The two most remarkable pieces from the Baroda treasury were auctioned by Sotheby's in 2009: the Pearl Carpet, in Doha on 19 March, and the Pearl Canopy, in New York on 24 March. The Pearl Carpet and Canopy of Baroda are outstanding examples of the artistry and opulence of the treasures of the former princely states of India. The two items were commissioned in 1865 by Khande Rao Gaekwar of Baroda and were intended as a gift for the tomb of Muhammad in Medina. The Carpet is embroidered with at least one-and-a-half million Basra pearls, which were sourced from the southern Gulf, and further decorated with table-cut diamonds, sapphires, emeralds and rubies set in gold (p. 202). The Canopy has a similar design but is circular, and is embellished with at least 500,000–650,000 Basra pearls and, as with the Carpet, at least 700 foil-backed rubies, emeralds and sapphires set in gold and no less than 200 table-cut diamonds set in silver and gold.

For centuries, India has been a rich source of diamonds and precious stones, which have often been surrounded by an aura of mystery. Few jewels and gemstones carry such a fabled provenance as those that were in the Baroda treasury and it was thanks to the Maharani Sita Devi that European high society glimpsed something of the splendour that at one time characterized the princely courts of India. ✳

Maria Callas

9

'Here she comes, the Queen of Sheba! She's the Empress of China and all the Russias! She's the Queen of Spain! She's Cleopatra! She's Aida. Double the trumpets. Increase the brass! Here are all the queens and empresses rolled into one! Who could resist such a voice! Hypnotized, my ship sped straight on, crashing to smithereens on the reefs of the Lorelei! I was in love!'

With these words, Yves Saint Laurent captured the essence of Maria Callas as a woman and as an artist. Throughout his life, the designer kept in his bedroom a portrait of the singer in the lead role of Verdi's masterpiece, *La Traviata*. He was one of thousands of Callas's admirers all over the globe. La Divina, as she was known, was a phenomenon that transcended the world of opera to become one of the great icons of the last century.

Maria Callas was born Maria Kalogeropoulos (her father later shortened his surname to Kalos and then Callas) in New York on 2 December 1923. Her parents had emigrated with her sister, Jackie, to the United States from Athens only four months before her birth. They had decided to begin a new life after their son, Vasily, died of typhoid in 1922, a tragedy that put enormous strain on the couple's relationship. Maria's childhood was scarred by a lack of affection from her mother, Evangelina, who had hoped for another son and consequently never accepted her. In later years, her mother considered her an ugly duckling when compared with her beautiful sister.

From an early age, however, Maria revealed a musical talent and was made to sing by her mother. She later felt that this pressure to perform had robbed her of her childhood. In 1937, Evangelina moved back to Athens with her two daughters, and in 1940 Maria became a pupil of Elvira de Hidalgo at the Athens Conservatoire. The great Spanish coloratura soprano detected the enormous potential in the young girl and shaped her future singing technique. By nature, Maria Callas had a potent voice with the depth of a mezzo soprano. De Hidalgo decided to train her as a soprano *drammatico d'agilità*, with the aim of softening her voice and rendering it more fluid and accurate. Maria herself would admit later in an interview: 'My timbre was dark, blackish, and complicated by the limitations in the upper register.' But with the adept guidance of her teacher, the young singer's voice developed in range to span three octaves, allowing her to perform with the light coloratura of a bel canto soprano as well as with the dramatic lyrical agility of a mezzo soprano. With this extraordinary ability she was able to sing an extensive repertoire that embraced three centuries of opera music.

The youthful Callas made her operatic debut in Athens in a student production of Mascagni's *Cavalleria Rusticana* and thanks to De Hildago began to get roles with the Greek National Opera. In 1942, she made her debut in a leading role in Puccini's *Tosca* and later played Leonore in Beethoven's *Fidelio*. By the end of the war she had been in seven operas. Once the hostilities were over, she returned to the United States, but once there she met with a series of difficulties in breaking into the world of professional opera.

Her luck changed in the summer of 1947 when, thanks to a recommendation from her friend the bass Nicola Rossi-Lemeni, she made her Italian debut in the title role in Amilcare Ponchielli's *La Gioconda* at the Arena di Verona. The performance was under the direction of the famous maestro Tullio Serafin but though Maria was well received, no one would ever have imagined that this young and overweight woman

Page 204
Maria Callas, photographed by
Cecil Beaton in 1957, wearing
her diamond and pearl pendent
earrings.

Her *cinq feuilles* ruby and
diamond brooch by Van Cleef
& Arpels, 1967.

Right
Callas at a party in her honour,
at the Royal Albert Hall in
London on 3 February 1957.
She is wearing a late-1940s
diamond scroll brooch (far right)
on her ermine hat and diamond
cascade pendent earrings by
Van Cleef & Arpels.

with the unusual voice would become 'the Divine'. The
meeting with Serafin was crucial for the development
of her career, but she also met Giovanni Battista
Meneghini in Verona, an opera-loving industrialist
twenty years her senior who was to become her
manager and two years later, in 1949, her husband.

In January 1949, Callas was in Venice to sing the
role of Brünnhilde in Wagner's *Die Walküre*, under the
direction of Serafin. He was also directing Bellini's
I Puritani, with the famous coloratura soprano
Margherita Carosio as Elvira. Carosio, however, fell
ill and Serafin urgently needed a replacement. At the
hotel where the maestro and Maria were both staying,
he heard her playing the piano and singing a coloratura
piece. Realizing the exceptional qualities of Callas's
voice, he invited her to take on the role of Elvira, which
she learned in two days. The extraordinary versatility
she displayed of being able to sing both Brünnhilde
and Elvira within a matter of days marked a turning

point in her career; thereafter, with the help of Serafin,
she moved away from the heavier roles in the repertoire
to those of the earlier Italian operas.

The true Callas phenomenon, however, exploded
at La Scala in Milan. Her first role there was in April
1950, when she substituted for Renata Tebaldi in the
last three performances of *Aida* that season. Tebaldi,
described by Arturo Toscanini as having 'the voice of
an angel', was the antithesis of Maria Callas. They
would become great rivals, giving rise to numerous
articles in the press and dividing opera lovers into two
groups: the 'Callasiani', or Callas fans, and the
'Tebaldiani', or Tebaldi fans. Soon, Tebaldi, upstaged
by Callas with her versatile voice, left La Scala to
become one of the leading singers at the Metropolitan
Opera House, New York.

Callas was now free to rule over La Scala uncon-
tested, and did so through the 1950s. She played
twenty-three roles there and sang in almost 200

performances, many of which contributed to forging her legend. She was also a great favourite at Covent Garden, where she made her debut in November 1952 in *Norma*.

As her success at La Scala grew, Maria realized that she was too heavy to perform with the intensity that the tragic heroines she was called to interpret required. With the same single-minded determination that she had used to shape her voice into one of the most extraordinary instruments in the history of opera, she lost more than 30 kilos, transforming herself from an ugly duckling into an elegant and sophisticated swan, although the effect on her voice is disputed.

In 1954, after Callas had had several successes at La Scala, the management was happy to put on new productions for her. She suggested that *La Vestale*, an opera by Gaspare Spontini that had not been in the repertoire for twenty-five years, be brought back for her. The direction was given to Luchino Visconti; it was the first opera that he had ever staged. The new production was a particularly lavish one. Visconti recognized the intensity of Callas's personality and

Callas at the Hilton Hotel in Chicago, November 1954, for a dinner in her honour after the performance of *Norma*. This was her American debut. She is followed (left) by her husband, Giovanni Battista Meneghini, and (right) by her father, George.

Left
A pair of diamond and natural pearl pendent earrings. The design is a brilliant-cut stylized ribbon motif, centred by a line of baguette diamonds from which the two pear-shaped, slightly irregular natural pearls are suspended.

Far left
Callas wearing the two pearls in their original antique setting.

Opposite
Callas wearing the two pearls in their modern setting, in a studio portrait by Cecil Beaton in 1957.

the potential to channel it into her interpretations, and succeeded in refining her instincts as an actress. He also taught her impeccable manners and deportment, turning her into a sophisticated, high-society lady. Her ideal of beauty was Audrey Hepburn, of whom she kept a photograph in her dressing room.

One can build an image of Callas from the description by the journalist Carla Maria Casanova, who became passionate about opera when she was a girl after she heard a Callas performance on the radio. She was so moved by Callas's voice that she persuaded her parents to take her to see the singer on stage and on 17 December 1955 they went to a performance of *Norma* at La Scala. After that, Casanova never missed one of Callas's roles at La Scala. She saw Donizetti's *Anna Bolena* seven times and Umberto Giordano's *Fedora* five times. Later, she would travel to see Maria in operas and concerts abroad, including ones in Edinburgh, Brussels, Amsterdam and Epidaurus. Looking back, she summed up the artist:

> Maria Callas had an extraordinary theatrical impact and her singing was perfectly suited to the music, the situations

and the roles that she interpreted. Her diction was perfect: extremely intense, with every syllable distinct and filled with meaning. Her whole body sang, from her short-sighted eyes, with which she was unable to see the conductor, to her beautiful hands: long nervous, expressive, sensual. There was no role performed by Callas in which she did not leave a strong impression – so much so that it is impossible to separate her from each one she interpreted. It is difficult nowadays to find the same emotion when you see *Norma*, *Medea*, *Lucia*, *Fedora*, *Anna Bolena* … I remember when she was still heavy; Maria had a beautiful face with soft lines and an important nose, but her body was heavy and clumsy. After a rigorous diet, her facial features became exaggerated: big nose, big mouth, enormous eyes in which contact lenses mitigated her myopic expression. But the fluidity of her body and her harmonious posture, the well-executed makeup and sophisticated elegance transformed her into an icon. A woman of enormous fascination; maybe really beautiful.

Callas now had the figure of a model and her new image was enhanced by the renowned Milanese couturier 'Biki' (Elvira Leonardi Bouyeure) who would not only become her fashion designer but also a lifelong

friend. Biki created the most magnificent wardrobe for Maria, down to the smallest detail. Now, she not only had a superb voice and the perfect physique to perform on stage, but had also acquired the magnetic appeal of an attractive woman.

With her new figure and sophisticated clothes, all that Callas needed to complete her look was some magnificent jewelry. Meneghini had given her some attractive diamond jewels in the late 1940s but they now began to look outdated. One of those pieces was a diamond brooch of scroll design (p. 206) that must have had a special significance for Maria because she treasured it all her life. Meneghini gave her beautiful jewels to commemorate each success in her career. For her triumphant performance in Cherubini's *Medea* at La Scala in December 1953, conducted by Leonard Bernstein, he bought her a ruby and diamond *parure* comprising a necklace, bracelet and ear clips (pp. 211 and 221). This set was bought in Milan, at Faraone, which was one of the most esteemed jewelers of the time and famous for selling the work of Harry Winston. Indeed, these pieces are typical of his jewelry. Callas loved this elegant suite and wore it at countless official events as well as on stage. It is worth noting that the opening of each season at La Scala was a major occasion for society ladies to exhibit their magnificent jewels, and many jewelry firms established important contacts there.

In January 1954, Callas's performance in the leading role of Donizetti's *Lucia di Lammermoor*, under the direction of Herbert von Karajan, was another triumph that caused a musical revolution. In the final scene of Lucia's descent into madness, the intensity of Callas's singing was mesmerising. To commemorate this new milestone in her career, Meneghini gave the diva a diamond necklace with a matching ring and also a stylish diamond bracelet. As with the ruby and diamond *parure*, she was photographed wearing the set on and off stage during the 1950s, but this one does not appear in photographs after the 1960s.

The artistic marriage of Callas and Visconti gave birth, in May 1955, to a new production of Verdi's *La Traviata*. The performance was very modern and different from previous stagings, and Visconti's direction provoked much debate among opera lovers. But Callas's sensitive interpretation and her sound, with the light coloratura voice she used for the first act and the dramatic colours she gave to the rest, was sublime. Despite what the critics said, nearly sixty years later this *Traviata* remains the benchmark by which subsequent performances are judged. On this occasion, her husband gave Callas a full emerald and diamond *parure* comprising a necklace, bangle, pendent earrings and an extraordinary ring set with a step-cut emerald weighing 37.56 cts (pp. 211, 214 and 215).

Maria Callas's American debut took place in Chicago in November 1954 and just under two years later, on 29 October 1956, she made her first appearance at the Metropolitan Opera House in New York, in Bellini's *Norma*. The ticket sales that evening broke the box-office's records: *The New York Times* observed that 'never had so many Americans tried to pay so much to hear an opera'. The night of her debut at the Met, Callas attended a party in her honour in the Trianon Room of the Ambassador Hotel. She arrived an hour after midnight, dressed magnificently in a ruby red velvet evening gown and ermine and adorned with a spectacular array of diamonds worth over a million dollars that had been lent to her for the occasion by Harry Winston. Appearing in all the most fashionable magazines, Callas was the best form of publicity for any jeweler. The party's guest list read like a musical and social 'who's who', including fellow stars such as Marlene Dietrich. One man never took his eyes off the diva: the private detective hired by Winston to safeguard the valuable jewels. The necklace was particularly stunning, designed as a diamond *rivière* from which hung a large marquise-shaped diamond and a pear-shaped diamond. It was accompanied by matching pendent earrings and a ring. This party might be regarded as the event when Callas began to move from being an opera star to a member of the beau monde.

At about this time, Maria met Elsa Maxwell, the famous gossip columnist and party organizer for the

Callas photographed in December 1957 admiring the jewels given to her by her husband, Giovanni Battista Meneghini, to celebrate her career successes, including, on the cushion, the diamond necklace, ring and bracelet she received for *Lucia di Lammermoor*. She is wearing the ruby and diamond *parure* that celebrated her performance in *Medea*, and she is admiring the 37.56 cts emerald ring that, together with a necklace, bangle and pendent earrings, honoured her role as Violetta in *La Traviata*.

Above
An emerald and diamond
necklace by Harry Winston, from
the mid-1950s. This necklace
is one of several pieces that
Harry Winston lent to Callas for
the Imperial Ball at the Waldorf
Astoria in New York in 1957 and
for photo sessions.

Top and centre
A marquise-shaped diamond
weighing 11.71 cts and diamond
ear clips, probably by Harry
Winston, which were given to
Callas by her husband in 1957.

Opposite left
Callas dressed as an Egyptian
queen for the Imperial Ball at
the Waldorf-Astoria in New York,
January 1957. The newspapers
reported that she wore jewels lent
by Harry Winston that were worth
over three million dollars.

Opposite right
Callas meeting former King
Umberto II of Italy on 10 July
1959 at the Amstel Hotel in
Amsterdam. She is wearing
a floral diamond brooch and
holding her beloved poodle, Toy,
who always travelled with her.

social elite all over the world. Maxwell, who up to that point had been a great friend and supporter of Callas's rival Renata Tebaldi, was transfixed. The following day she wrote in her column: 'When I looked into her amazing eyes, which are brilliant, beautiful, and hypnotic, I realized she is an extraordinary person.' The columnist was infatuated with the diva and started to invite her to her lavish parties, valuing the allure the singer added to her guest list. For Callas, the comforting mother figure (Maxwell was born in 1881) seems to have filled a need in her life. In January 1957, Maria attended the Imperial Ball at the Waldorf-Astoria in New York dressed as the Egyptian queen Hatshepshut. Her exotic costume was embellished with emerald and diamond jewelry lent to her for the occasion, once again by Harry Winston. Maxwell made sure that Callas was the star of the evening.

In the same year, Callas acquired a very elegant pair of diamond ear clips, designed as a cluster of brilliant-cut and pear-shaped diamonds. The total diamond weight was almost 29 cts. She also had a brooch to match the ear clips. The elegant platinum prong setting and the quality of the diamonds were typical of Harry Winston's work.

In April 1957, the conductor Gianandrea Gavazzeni resurrected *Anna Bolena* as a tribute to its composer, Donizetti. This opera had not been in the Italian repertoire since 1881, and Gavazzeni recognized in its leading role a part perfectly suited to Maria's talents, both musically and theatrically. Again, the direction was by Luchino Visconti – a man who fascinated Maria personally and professionally. Visconti knew how to bring out the sublime in her performance, and she followed all his suggestions. Everything in this new production was carefully designed to provide a perfect backdrop for Maria's sumptuous costumes and her vibrant interpretation of the tragic queen. As predicted by Gavazzeni, the opera was a tremendous success. In fact, the applause for Callas lasted twenty-four minutes at the end of the first performance, the record for a solo curtain call at La Scala. Later the same year, Callas and Visconti collaborated for the fifth, and last, time, on Gluck's *Iphigénie en Tauride*.

Meneghini marked these triumphs with another extraordinary gift to his wife: a ring claw-set with a colourless marquise-shaped diamond weighing 11.71 cts, which became another of her favourite pieces (p. 212). Later she would receive, to match the ring, a

Below
A ring set with a step-cut
emerald weighing 37.56 cts
between crossed shoulders
set with baguette diamonds.

Right
Callas wearing the emerald ring
at a ball in her honour in Venice,
September 1957. Her hostess,
the columnist Elsa Maxwell, and
Merle Oberon are also pictured.

Opposite
The emerald and diamond
necklace given to Callas by
her husband to celebrate her
success in *La Traviata* at La Scala
in May 1955.

bracelet composed of a line of marquise-shaped diamonds (p. 226). Also in the mid-1950s, Maria had her pearl-drop earrings updated from their antique setting. The new design was typical of the period: a stylized ribbon set with circular-cut diamonds from which hangs a line of baguette diamonds terminating in a pear-shaped natural pearl (p. 208). She wore these pendent earrings in concert performances and at social events. In the same period, she acquired a pair of pendent ear clips created by Van Cleef & Arpels as an articulated cascade of brilliant-cut diamonds (p. 225);

she would cherish them for the rest of her life. A stylish gold and diamond evening bag, also from Van Cleef & Arpels, was given to her by her husband in 1957 (p. 223). These pieces formed the beginning of Callas's strong relationship with the French firm.

In September 1957, Elsa Maxwell organized a ball in Venice in the diva's honour. As one of the events surrounding the Venice Film Festival, the guest list glittered with stars, but the occasion provoked controversy. Immediately before the party, Maria had appeared with the La Scala company at the Edinburgh Festival,

staring as Amina in Bellini's *La Sonnambula*. She had committed to four performances but the director of La Scala, Antonio Ghiringhelli, announced a fifth performance, which clashed with the Venice ball, without consulting her. She refused to perform and left for Venice. The British press and public, unaware of the full facts, severely criticised what to them was a diva-like attitude.

Despite the adverse publicity, Maxwell felt that she had never hosted a better dinner or ball. The ladies had to wear fancy headdresses, with a prize awarded by Maria for the best one. She herself wore two Van Cleef & Arpels diamond 'flamme' brooches in her hair and an emerald and diamond necklace, a piece that she was seen wearing in this period but, as with many others, she had abandoned by the 1960s. She also proudly wore the lapel pin indicating the honorary title of Commendatore recently awarded to her by the President of Italy for her artistic achievements.

The Venice ball had another significance for Callas: it was the occasion when Maxwell introduced the singer to one of the richest men in the world, the Greek

Right
A diamond necklace by Van Cleef & Arpels, 1958, designed as a double row of baguette and brilliant-cut diamonds with a pear-shaped diamond weighing 38 cts.

Below
Callas in the Van Cleef & Arpels shop in Paris in December 1958 trying on the necklace and pendent earrings that the firm would lend her for a charity concert in aid of the Légion d'honneur at the Palais Garnier – her Paris debut.

Opposite
Callas being congratulated by French President René Coty at the concert at the Palais Garnier, 19 December 1958.

shipping magnate Aristotle Onassis. The encounter was to determine the course of her subsequent life.

Meanwhile, just as she was enjoying enormous social success, Callas's singing career was running into problems. The weight loss and exhausting lifestyle, both on and off the stage, took their toll on her health and strained her voice. Her doctors suggested that she take some time to recuperate and she cancelled many artistic engagements. In an interview in later years she said, 'I had to defend myself all my life'; the press had constructed an image of Callas as a strong and feisty woman, who as a consequence was nicknamed 'the tiger', and the cancelled performances fuelled their portrayal of her as a socialite diva. In reality, the singer was craving the love that she had never received as a child; for her the 'jet set' helped to provide it.

Callas's ill health revealed itself with unfortunate consequences on the evening of 2 January 1958 at a gala performance of *Norma* at the opera house in Rome in front of the President of Italy and leading figures of Rome society. Maria's voice had started to trouble her the month before: she had successfully performed in Verdi's *Un Ballo in Maschera* for the opening of La Scala on 7 December but knew that her voice would have to be rested after the final performance on 22 December. She tried to cancel the *Norma* engagement in Rome but to no avail: tickets for the evening had sold out. Though she suggested that the director find a substitute in case her voice failed her, no replacement was found. Sadly, her fears were confirmed. During the first act, she was heckled by the audience; after it, she felt so ill that she stopped the performance. The 'Rome Walkout' was reported all over the world and although the opera house was later found culpable for

not providing an understudy, the event had damaged her career. In May 1958, she sang the role of Imogene in Bellini's *Il Pirata*, conducted by Antonino Votto, at La Scala but quarrelled with the general director Ghiringhelli who, after the Edinburgh incident, no longer regarded her as the queen of opera. Her touching performance rescued *Il Pirata* from oblivion and the public gave Callas a standing ovation. Nonetheless, she said she would not sing again at La Scala while Ghiringhelli was in charge.

She continued to appear elsewhere, however. In early June, she sang at a gala celebration to mark the centenary of Covent Garden and was graciously treated by the management, which included the Queen's cousin Lord Harewood. After two months rest at her home

Callas at the Monte Carlo Opera House with the Maharani of Baroda on 23 November 1960. She is wearing her favourite pearl pendent earrings.

in Sirmione, on the shores of Lake Garda, she did a concert tour of the United States and appeared at Dallas Civic Opera. But she suffered the same fate at the Metropolitan as she had at La Scala: she fell out of favour with its director, Rudolph Bing, and he terminated her contract.

This year of mixed fortune ended with a huge success: her debut in Paris on 19 December at a charity gala concert for the Légion d'honneur at the Palais Garnier in front of President René Coty and many other important guests. These included the Duke and Duchess of Windsor, the latter with ruby and diamond jewels by Van Cleef & Arpels glittering on her white dress; the Begum Aga Khan, also in white, wearing her Bulgari turquoise and diamond parure; Princess Maria Pia of Savoy, wearing a blue Balmain gown and emerald and diamond pendent earrings from the collection of Grand Duchess Vladimir of Russia, together with her husband, Prince Alexander of Yugoslavia; Prince Aly Khan with the model Bettina; Jean Cocteau and Françoise Sagan; Brigitte Bardot with Sacha Distel, Charlie Chaplin, Alain Delon, Yves Saint Laurent and, once again, Aristotle Onassis.

The concert was broadcast throughout Europe by French television. In the first half, Callas sang arias from *Norma*, *Il Trovatore* and *Il Barbiere di Siviglia* and was resplendent in a red velvet gown created for her by Biki. The magnificent jewels that she wore – diamond pendent earrings with a suspended diamond pear-shaped drop, an exceptional diamond *rivière* and a step-cut diamond ring – were lent to her by Van Cleef & Arpels for the occasion. The full second act of *Tosca* followed the interval. Callas's yellow dress, another Biki creation, was richly embroidered and trimmed with sable, and provided the perfect backdrop for a cabochon emerald and diamond necklace with matching earrings.

For the gala dinner in the foyer of the Palais Garnier after the concert, attended by 450 selected guests, the diva wore another Van Cleef & Arpels creation: a necklace composed of two rows of baguette and brilliant-cut diamonds supporting a large pear-shaped diamond (p. 216). After this, the firm would frequently lend her outstanding jewels when she needed to embellish her elegant gown for an important event. She would always be a loyal client. After the concert the compliments flooded in: on 22 December she received

Maria Callas and Aristotle
Onassis at an event in Majorca,
Spain, in July 1961. She is
wearing her cluster diamond ear
clips and matching brooch.

Right
A brooch by Van Cleef &
Arpels, 1968, in sapphires and
diamonds, identical to one
created for Callas.

Opposite
The ruby and diamond *parure* purchased at Faraone in Milan in 1953 after the singer's triumphant performance in *Medea* at La Scala. It is probably a piece of Harry Winston's, since Faraone was selling his creations in this period: the design and workmanship, and the quality of the stones, are characteristic of the famous New York jeweler.

Callas and Onassis photographed in December 1965. She is wearing her coral, turquoise, pearl and diamond bracelet and matching ear clips, a gift from Onassis.

Right
Callas wearing her favourite ruby and diamond *parure*, together with her diamond cascade pendent earrings, at Maxim's restaurant in Paris, celebrating the première of the movie *Zorba the Greek* with Baron Alexis de Redé and Baroness Marie-Hélène de Rothschild, 1965.

a telegram from the Begum Aga Khan, stating 'You were last Friday more divine than ever/to hear you is a pleasure of heavens/am most grateful/with best wishes for new year your great admirer Om Habibeh Aga Khan.'

In June 1959, Callas was back at Covent Garden performing in *Medea*. After the performance on 17 June Onassis organized a reception in her honour at the Dorchester Hotel. The tycoon was now completely besotted with the singer and courted her even though he was married. At this point, she was in a vulnerable state. She was 35 years old and in search of real passion

in her life. Her relationship with Meneghini had been damaged by the recent setbacks to her career, since he was also her manager. A turning point came when Onassis invited the Meneghinis on a cruise aboard his yacht *Christina*. Callas hesitated but her husband persuaded her to accept and on 2 July they set sail from Monte Carlo for Istanbul, together with a group of important people, including Sir Winston and Lady Churchill. Perhaps the singer should have followed her instincts and not gone on the trip, because in the course of the voyage she fell desperately in love with Onassis, spending hours talking with him in Greek.

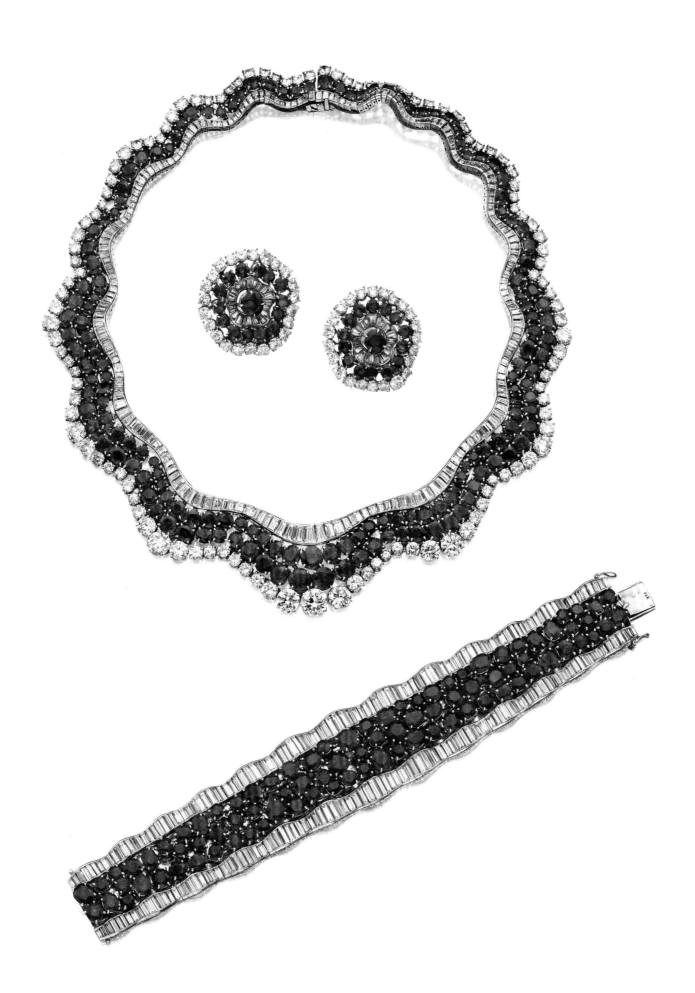

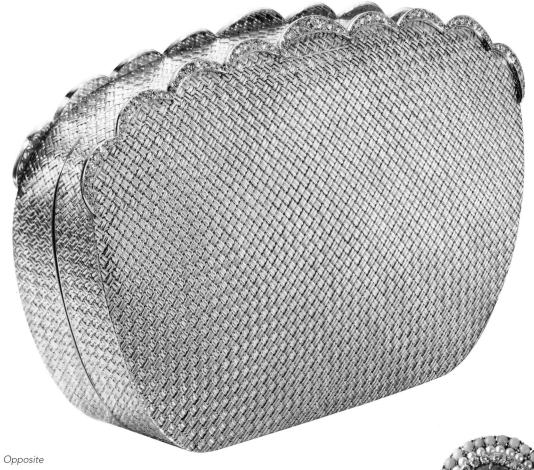

Opposite
Callas arriving at a reception in London in 1965. In her hand she holds the gold and diamond evening bag by Van Cleef & Arpels (above), and she wears the coral, diamond, pearl and turquoise ear clips (right).

Ear clips and bracelet in coral, pearl, diamond and turquoise: part of a set including a brooch. These ear clips and bracelet are the only jewels recorded as being a gift from Aristotle Onassis. He received them from Van Cleef & Arpels on 15 November 1965; they were probably intended as a gift for Callas's birthday on 2 December.

After the cruise she told her husband that she wanted a separation and in November they parted. The relationship between the two most famous Greeks in the world caused a huge scandal. It also completely took over the great artist, who at last felt loved even if she did not sing, as Onassis did not care much for opera.

Callas honoured the rest of her contracts for 1959, including performing again in *Lucia di Lammermoor* and *Medea* in Dallas. In August 1960, she had an enormous success in Greece singing *Norma* at the ancient theatre in Epidaurus under the direction of her loyal friend and mentor Serafin. It particularly pleased the artist that each night her father, George, joined the audience of over fifteen thousand people who had come from all over Greece. For Onassis, the event was significant as it marked the diva's return to Greece, with him at her side.

The couple's social life was now followed by the press all over the world. On 3 September, with the *Christina* anchored in the Bay of Naples, they attended the 'royal ball' thrown by the Duke Francesco and Duchess Elena Serra di Cassano at the Palazzo Pizzofalcone in Naples. Callas, as reported by Elsa Maxwell in her column, not only broke with convention by wearing a short dress but also did not wear any jewelry – in contrast to her friend the Maharani of Baroda who was dripping in rubies and diamonds.

Although her professional engagements were more infrequent, on 7 December 1960, after an absence of over two and a half years, Callas returned to La Scala, singing Paolina in *Poliuto* by Donizetti. The opening night of the season was always eagerly anticipated, not least for the display of jewelry and glamour, but this occasion was particularly sensational. Prince Rainier

Opposite
An emerald and diamond necklace by Van Cleef & Arpels, *c.*1966, designed as a double *rivière* of brilliant-cut diamonds and oval-shaped emeralds with a pear-shaped emerald in a brilliant-cut floral motif. Callas is wearing the necklace, together with her emerald pendent earrings, in the photograph. She is with Aristotle Onassis at the première of the revue *Pourquoi Pas?* at the Lido cabaret, Paris, 20 December 1966.

Right
Callas wearing her ruby and diamond *parure* together with her brilliant-cut diamond cascade ear pendants at the première of the film *Phèdre* in October 1968 in Paris. She is with Yves Saint Laurent and Hélène Rochas.

Brilliant-cut diamond cascade pendent earrings by Van Cleef & Arpels from the 1950s. In 1967, Callas had the firm alter the setting by placing large brilliant-cut diamonds as the last four stones of each line, as illustrated here.

and Princess Grace of Monaco were present, as well as the Begum Aga Khan, as Onassis's guests. The high-profile audience and the pressure of returning to the theatre that had made her a legend, made Callas extremely nervous and the reviews were critical. From now on, as the singer made fewer appearances, the attention each performance received increased, which only heightened the tension for her. Henceforth, she sang only *Medea*, *Norma* and *Tosca* on stage.

In August 1961, she had another huge success at Epidaurus, this time in *Medea*, but Onassis was not with her as he was a restless man, always on the move, looking after his business interests. In December, she sang in three performances of the same opera at La Scala, with two further appearances in May and June of 1962. Those were the last occasions on which she sang in the theatre that had brought her so much glory.

Callas continued to give occasional concerts in Europe but her appearances tended to be scheduled around cruises on the *Christina* and her life as a member of the jet set. She spent less time practising and her voice was suffering. But so was her relationship with Onassis. He was no longer quite so passionate about the great diva and as she reached 40 she realized that she was missing the most important element of her life: the world of opera. In January 1964, she returned to Covent Garden in a celebrated production of *Tosca*, directed by Franco Zeffirelli, with Tito Gobbi playing Scarpia. Her voice was not what it had been but she still knew how to project magic on stage and the second act was shown on British television. Her rejuvenated career continued at the Palais Garnier in Paris with *Norma* in May and nine performances of *Tosca* in February 1965. The diva was reconciled with Bing at the Met in New York and received a touching welcome from her fans there when she returned to sing twice in *Tosca* with Gobbi in March. Five performances of *Norma* in Paris in May exhausted her and she cancelled all her scheduled appearances in *Tosca* at Covent Garden bar one. So the very last time Callas sang a full opera was on 5 July 1965 at Covent Garden at a gala evening

Callas in a studio portrait in 1964. She is wearing a diamond spray brooch and a bracelet designed as a line of marquise-shaped diamonds.

Right
The marquise-shaped bracelet mounted to be used as a necklace, with brilliant-cut and navette diamonds taken from the old settings of her emerald and diamond bangle and pendent earrings. Van Cleef & Arpels consigned the final version to her in 1973.

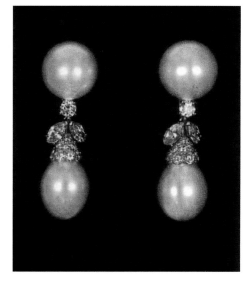

Above
The cultured pearl and diamond pendent earrings from Van Cleef & Arpels that Callas acquired in October 1971.

Left
Callas wearing the pearl and diamond pendent earrings after one of her concerts, November 1973. She is being congratulated by Elizabeth Taylor who is wearing the pearl, ruby and diamond necklace that Cartier created to suspend the magnificent 'La Peregrina' pearl, which Richard Burton had bought for her.

Right
A panther brooch realized in yellow gold with black enamel spots and pear-shaped emerald eyes; the animal is reclining over a carved agate. It was created by Cartier, Paris, in 1972 and acquired in the same year by Callas.

in aid of the Royal Opera House Benevolent Fund in the presence of Queen Elizabeth II and other members of the royal family.

For the most part, it is not known which jewels Maria was given by Onassis. In 1965, however, he gave her, possibly for her birthday, a pair of ear clips and a bracelet set with round cabochon coral in a triple cluster of diamonds, pearls and turquoises (p. 223); a combination of colours that was extremely fashionable at the time. In the same year, Maria acquired a pair of ruby and diamond 'pelouse' ear clips. In 1967, she had her cascade diamond pendent earrings altered by Van Cleef & Arpels with larger brilliant-cut diamonds set as the last four stones of each line (p. 225).

Maria had hoped to marry Onassis but their relationship was becoming increasingly strained and they began to live separate lives. The final blow came when the tycoon married Jackie Kennedy on 20 October 1968. Maria was devastated. She found some distraction the following year when the filmmaker Pier Paolo

Cultured pearl and diamond *sautoir* necklace made for Callas by Van Cleef & Arpels in 1974. The back section can be used as a bracelet; the central lion's head motif was set with brilliant-cut diamonds.

Opposite
Callas being greeted by fans at the Théâtre des Champs-Elysées in Paris on the occasion of her last European concert, 8 December 1973. She is wearing the ruby and diamond *cinq feuilles* brooch created by Van Cleef & Arpels in 1967, as well as ruby and diamond chandelier pendent ear clips.

Pasolini cast her in his film *Medea*. At the première in January 1970 she wore an extraordinary pair of emerald and diamond pendent earrings with a matching brooch, again lent by Van Cleef & Arpels.

The same year, she instructed the firm to remount the emeralds from her pendent earrings and bangle. The pear-shaped emeralds, weighing 3.83 and 3.51 cts respectively, were reset in a cluster of navette diamonds as ear clips. The square cushion-shaped emerald of 15.90 cts was removed from the diamond bangle in which it was set at the centre and mounted in a cluster of brilliant-cut and navette diamonds in a stylish ring. The mounts were made of platinum with the prongs for the emeralds in yellow gold. The old settings were returned to Maria.

In October 1971, the diva bought a pair of Van Cleef & Arpels cultured pearl and diamond pendent earrings (p. 227). They became one of her favourite pieces, which she loved to wear with a single row of South Sea cultured pearls. In 1972, Maria acquired a Cartier panther brooch made of yellow gold, enamel, emeralds and agate (p. 227), and later that year she took the old settings of her emerald pendent earrings and bangle to Van Cleef & Arpels in New York. The brilliant-cut and navette diamonds from these pieces were mounted with her marquise-shaped diamond *rivière* bracelet so that she could also wear it as a necklace (p. 226). It was delivered in February 1973.

Maria had not performed but given some master classes at the Juilliard School in New York in this period. However, in 1973 she was contacted by the tenor Giuseppe di Stefano, her partner in many operas, who proposed a concert tour together. She had lost her voice but with her single-minded focus she started to retrain it and in the process she seemed to regain her enthusiasm for life. She and Di Stefano toured all over the world in 1973–74 and although musically not a great success because both singers were past their peak, the concerts were extremely popular. Photographs of the events show Callas beaming and the public delighted to see the return of their living legend.

For the concert at the Théâtre des Champs-Elysées on 8 December 1973, Callas wore a flowing chiffon red dress embellished with a Van Cleef & Arpels ruby and diamond *cinq feuilles* brooch, from 1967 (p. 204). She had ruby and diamond pendent ear clips to accompany the brooch. In this period she treated herself to other

acquisitions from Van Cleef & Arpels, including a pearl and diamond *sautoir* necklace made for her in 1974, composed of three strands of cultured pearls with a foliate connection – in yellow gold and accented with brilliant-cut diamonds – to a central lion's head motif set with brilliant-cut diamonds, from which a cultured pearl tassel was suspended (p. 228). The necklace could be shortened and a section used as a bracelet. In 1975, she bought a pair of double 'boule' ear clips set in yellow gold, *pavé*-set with brilliant-cut diamonds, which she loved to wear with her pearl and diamond necklace.

The concert tour finished in Japan on 11 November 1974 and she returned to Paris, where she became increasingly isolated, suffered from depression and needed pills to help her sleep. On 15 March 1975 her great love, Aristotle Onassis, with whom she had remained close, died in a Paris hospital and in November the same year Pier Paolo Pasolini, whom she regarded as an important friend, was murdered in Italy. Then on 17 March 1976, her mentor and friend Luchino Visconti died.

On 16 September 1977, Maria Callas collapsed and died in Paris, probably from a heart attack brought about by the abuse of pills. She was only 53. The funeral was held at St Stephen's Cathedral, the Greek Orthodox church in Paris, on 20 September, and was attended by hundreds of people, including Princess Grace of Monaco and her daughter Caroline. After initial burial in Père Lachaise cemetery, her ashes were scattered in the Aegean off the coast of Greece in 1979.

Some twenty-five years later, on 17 November 2004, a selection of jewels from Maria Callas's collection was offered at auction by Sotheby's in Geneva. The pieces that had marked so many triumphs in her career were there. Like her diamonds, the legend of Maria Callas will live forever. ✄

HH The Begum
Aga Khan III

10

On 15 November 2000, a group of magnificent jewels from the collection of Her Highness Begum Sultan Muhammad Shah Aga Khan was offered for sale at Sotheby's Geneva, in aid of the Aga Khan Foundation. The Begum, who was the fourth wife of the Aga Khan III, and his widow for over forty years, had died some four months earlier at the age of 94. The photograph on the front of the catalogue portrayed an elegant lady with a radiant smile and an air of serene grace, but it conveyed little of an extraordinary life story.

The Begum had been born Yvette Blanche Labrousse on 15 February 1906 in Sète, near Montpellier, in the south of France, the daughter of a tram conductor and a seamstress. She grew into a tall and beautiful girl and in 1930 was crowned Miss France. She travelled to many countries and in the mid-1930s she met HH Sir Sultan Muhammad Shah Aga Khan III in Egypt. This was the beginning of one of the most romantic love stories of the 20th century.

The Aga Khan (a title conferred by the British on his grandfather) had been born in Karachi in 1877 and in 1885 succeeded his father as the spiritual and political head of the Shia Ismaili Muslims, a sect consisting of 11–12 million ethnically and culturally diverse peoples scattered across Asia, the Middle East and Africa. The Aga Khan, a descendant of the Prophet Muhammad, was the 48th Imam, a position he held for seventy-two years until his death in 1957. The role was temporal as well as spiritual and the Aga Khan's ancestors included the Fatimid Caliphs who had founded Cairo in the tenth century. He himself played an active part in politics, becoming the first president of the All-India Muslim League in 1906 and participated in negotiations with the British over the government of India. He was highly respected and became a figure on the internationtional diplomatic scene, serving as president of the League of Nations in 1937. The Aga Khan was also well known as a philanthropist, using his vast wealth to establish schools, hospitals and community programmes in Asia, the Middle East and Africa. At the outbreak of the Second World War, he encouraged his followers to support the Allied cause. In his sixties and suffering from ill health, he spent the war years in Switzerland receiving medical treatment.

Following his divorce in Geneva in 1943 from his third wife, the Aga Khan and Yvette Labrousse were married on 9 October 1944. He was twenty-eight years her senior but despite the age difference they were very compatible. In his memoirs, *World Enough and Time* (1954), he wrote: 'I can only say that if a perfectly happy marriage be one in which there is a genuine and complete union and understanding, on the spiritual, mental and emotional planes, ours is such.' Yvette had converted to Islam and took the name Om Habibeh (Little Mother of the Beloved) when she married. Out of respect for her new family, she frequently wore Indian saris, often with traditional Eastern jewelry, including bangles and large gold necklaces decorated with precious stones and multi-coloured enamels.

The Aga Khan was passionate about horse-racing and his studs had an outstanding record: he was named British flat-racing Champion Owner thirteen times and had five winners of the Epsom Derby. He gave HRH Princess Elizabeth a filly on the occasion of her marriage to Lt Philip Mountbatten in November 1947, and the horse, which she named Astrakhan, was her first winner on the flat. The Aga Khan and the Begum were a familiar sight at race courses in Europe: from Longchamps and Chantilly to Epsom and Ascot. She was photographed wearing stylish dresses and dazzling contemporary jewelry. Around her neck were strands

231

Opposite
The Aga Khan III and the Begum at Ascot on 14 July 1955. She is wearing a ruby and diamond brooch in the form of an exotic flower; it is also illustrated below with a matching ring.

Right
To mark the Aga Khan's diamond jubilee as leader of the Shia Ismaili Muslims he was given the equivalent of his weight (243 lbs) in diamonds in a ceremony at Brabourne Stadium in Mumbai on 10 March 1946. The stones, worth £640,000, were used to finance Ismaili good causes.

The Begum dressed in a sari and wearing a diamond necklace and bracelet from the late 1940s.

A dragonfly brooch by Lalique, *c.* 1900. The wings are set with *plique-à-jour* enamel and the body is formed from opals and diamonds.

of beautiful pearls and she often wore a brooch to complete her outfit. One of her favourite pieces was a ruby and diamond brooch designed as an exotic flower, which she also loved to wear in her hair. A matching ring complemented this jewel (left).

The Begum also accompanied her husband in performing his official duties. Among the more astonishing ceremonies of his Imamat were those that marked the golden (1937), diamond (1946) and platinum (1954) jubilees. On each occasion the Ismaili community matched his weight with the relevant metal or precious stone. At the diamond jubilee event in India, 243 lbs of diamonds worth £640,000 were put on the scales. The money raised from these celebrations was invested in Ismaili welfare and development programmes.

In 1898, as a young man newly arrived from India on the Côte d'Azur, the Aga Khan stared at the diamonds, rubies, emeralds and sapphires on display in jewelers' windows 'for the eyes of the wealthiest people in Europe', as he later recalled in his memoirs. He himself became a patron of Cartier from 1902 and commissioned some stunning pieces from the firm during the 1920s and 1930s. In 1927, he had some

emeralds and sapphires mounted in a fashionable *sautoir*.
A year later, he consigned for sale to Cartier thirty-
eight large circular diamonds and three pear-shaped
diamonds of 40, 38 and 35 cts respectively. With these
the firm created a spectacular *sautoir*: the circular stones
were connected by geometric motifs and the pear-
shaped diamonds became the pendant and clasp.
However, Cartier was unable to sell this expensive
necklace – it was the time of the Wall Street Crash – so
it was broken up and the circular stones were sold to
the King of Nepal. The largest pear-shaped stone was
given to Prince Aly Khan, the Aga Khan's son by his
second wife; the stone of 38 cts was returned to the
Aga Khan and, in later years, was recut into an inter-
nally flawless stone of 33.13 cts, which became known
as the Aga Khan III Diamond; the stone weighing
35 cts was retained by Cartier.

In 1930, the Aga Khan supplied Cartier with two
historic emeralds belonging to his family. They were
both engraved with a sura from the Qur'an: one, of 76
cts, was mounted on a bracelet of diamonds, engraved
emeralds and sapphires; the other, a cushion-shaped
emerald tablet of 142.20 cts, was mounted in diamonds
as a brooch/pendant. These jewels were inherited by
Prince Sadruddin, the Aga Khan's son by his third wife.
In keeping with the family's charitable work, he sold
them at Christie's Geneva in May 1988 in aid of the
Bellerive Foundation, which he established in 1977 to
fund environmental programmes.

The jewels sold in the 2000 sale of the Begum's
collection all dated from the late 1950s and 1960s. This
was not only because, like all stylish ladies of the time,
she periodically updated her jewelry, but also because
some of her jewels were stolen in 1949. In August that
year, the Aga Khan and the Begum had just left their
villa above Cannes on their way to Nice airport when
masked gunmen held up their car. One of the men
snatched the Begum's jewelry box, containing pieces
worth about £200,000, that she held on her lap, but
the couple were unharmed. As the thieves were running
away, the Aga Khan found his sense of humour and
shouted that they had forgotten their tip; one gunman
ran back and collected a handful of francs. In 1953,
three of the robbers were convicted and some of the
jewelry was recovered.

Among the Begum's jewels at the 2000 sale was
an elegant ring set with a step-cut diamond weighing

The Begum at police
headquarters checking some
jewels after thieves robbed the
couple in their car on the road
above Cannes in 1949.

Opposite
The Begum and the Aga Khan
with an unidentified woman,
photographed in Aix-en-Provence
in July 1950 by Robert Doisneau.
The Begum is wearing an array
of Indian jewels.

The Begum at Ascot in 1958, the year after the Aga Khan had died. She is wearing the two sapphire and diamond clip brooches illustrated below and her favourite five-strand cultured pearl necklace. The ring is set with a step-cut diamond, weighing 14.7 cts, and a step-cut sapphire, weighing 13.98 cts, between trapeze-shaped diamond shoulders.

14.7 cts and a step-cut sapphire weighing 13.98 cts between trapeze-shaped diamond shoulders. It accompanied two sapphire and diamond clips, which she often wore, designed as stylized flowerheads, one in the reverse colours of the other (p. 236). They were of French manufacture and unsigned but their unusual composition suggests the brooches were probably by Pierre Sterlé, whose dynamic style was liked by the Begum. One unusual example of his art was the Alexandre brooch, created in 1965 (below right). In the form of a warrior, it was one of a set of figures created between 1965 and 1974. The head was sculpted in haematite by Robert Lemoine, a well-known carver of fine stones, and the flowing movement of the body was fashioned from mother-of-pearl and gold, highlighted with diamonds and *calibré*-cut rubies. This unique piece was signed Chaumet because at the beginning of his career Sterlé designed and made jewels for other important French firms.

In about 1964 the Begum chose Sterlé to modify a turquoise and diamond necklace by Bulgari that she had acquired in the late 1950s. The original design had been in the style of a bib, with the emphasis on the front and a single line of stones at the back, but the Begum was dissatisfied with this. Sterlé's additions created a star pattern, which transformed the necklace into an extremely sophisticated and glamorous piece (p. 238). He designed a pair of ear clips to match. This suite became one of the Begum's favourites and she wore it to the My Fair Lady Ball, hosted by Hélène Rochas in Paris in 1965 (p. 239). At this gathering of international high society, each lady had to wear a headpiece. The Begum wore egret feathers and a velvet band decorated to great effect with a turquoise and diamond bracelet by Bulgari, which she bought in 1958 to complement the necklace. In 1965, Sterlé created a matching turquoise and diamond brooch in the shape of a loosely knotted ribbon (p. 240).

Begum Om Habibeh was known for her passion for classical music, especially opera; she travelled to important performances all over the world and was an admirer of Maria Callas. She was always a sought-after presence at La Scala in Milan, where she was a guest of the director of the theatre and was often accompanied by Wally Toscanini, daughter of the maestro. Her interest in the arts was not just as a spectator: she was a painter and, in particular, an accomplished sculptress.

Top
The Begum at Longchamp on 5 October 1952 with her husband's racehorse Nuccio, winner of the Prix de l'Arc de Triomphe.

Above
The Alexandre brooch, created in 1965 by Pierre Sterlé, set with mother-of-pearl *calibré*-cut rubies and diamonds.

Opposite
The Begum photographed by Raymond Depardon talking to Merle Oberon at the My Fair Lady Ball in Paris in 1965. She is wearing the turquoise and diamond *parure* with the bracelet used as a head ornament.

In the late 1950s the Begum acquired a necklace and bracelet in turquoise and diamonds by Bulgari. Pierre Sterlé altered the necklace in the early 1960s to the design shown here and created matching ear clips.

The original design drawing and the finished turquoise and diamond brooch created by Pierre Sterlé in 1965.

Opposite
The Aga Khan with his family in the South of France in 1949. Standing, left to right: Prince Amyn, younger son of Aly Khan; Prince Sadruddin and his half-brother, Prince Aly Khan, the Aga Khan's sons; Prince Karim, elder son of Aly Khan. Seated, left to right: the Begum, the Aga Khan and Rita Hayworth, who married Aly Khan in May that year.

She was grateful for the way in which her husband had broadened her horizons, and conscious of how fortunate she was. Her dignity, integrity and naturalness struck everyone she met in the course of her travels, not only when she was supporting her husband in his religious work and at sporting events, but also on social occasions, such as royal weddings, and on visits to the philanthropic programmes with which he was engaged. She took a particular interest in issues affecting women's welfare and would frequently be the guest of honour at fundraising events for charitable organizations.

The Begum cared for her husband devotedly through the ill health of his declining years. After his death in July 1957, she supervised the design and construction of his mausoleum on the banks of the Nile at Aswan, where the couple had bought a villa in 1954, having previously stayed one or two months annually at the Cataract Hotel. Thereafter, she spent part of

each year in Aswan and would place a single red rose on his tomb every day, or, if she was abroad, arrange for it to be done for her. Her sensitive nature was also revealed by her work to improve the living conditions in Aswan, whether through early childhood education or strengthening civil society organizations, and to further these endeavours she founded the Om Habibeh Foundation in 1991.

In choosing his successor, the Aga Khan broke with tradition and skipped a generation, so that instead of his son Aly Khan, it was Prince Karim, Aly Khan's elder son, who became the Aga Khan IV. He was only 20 and still a student at Harvard but, as it happened, he would have become the 49th Imam in any case, when his father was killed in a car crash in 1960. The Aga Khan suggested that the Begum should act as a counsellor to Karim for the first seven years of his Imamat, as she was familiar with the issues facing the Ismaili community and had excellent judgment. Throughout the rest of her life, she maintained good relations with Prince Karim Aga Khan IV, his brother, Prince Amyn, and their half-sister, Princess Yasmin, as well as with her step-son Prince Sadruddin, who was United Nations High Commissioner for Refugees, 1965–77.

After the death of the Aga Khan, the Begum divided her time between the house adjacent to the mausoleum in Aswan and her villa at Le Cannet in the South of France. The couple had built the house after the war in the hills above Cannes and called it Yakymour. The name derived from a combination of 'Yaky' (from the initial letters of Yvette Aga Khan) and 'amour'. In later years, she founded a retirement home in the town and in 1999 the mayor unveiled a bronze statue in her honour in the Jardin des Oliviers.

Through the Begum's long widowhood, she took part in many events in connection with the Ismaili community. She was always elegantly dressed and wore magnificent jewels. The only period piece included in the 2000 sale was a delicate dragonfly brooch by Lalique from *c.* 1900 that could also be worn as a hair ornament. The wings were decorated with pale blue *plique-à-jour* enamel and the body was set with opals and diamonds (p. 230). It still had its original case.

One of her favourite pieces was a five-strand cultured pearl necklace, which was sold together with a pair of cultured pearl and diamond pendent earrings (p. 242). She also wore those with a late-1960s diamond necklace. Its diamond and platinum setting was embellished with flowers in yellow gold, set with diamonds, bordered by a fringe of cultured pearl drops (p. 248).

Ear clips designed as a cluster surmount set with pear- and marquise-shaped and brilliant-cut diamonds, with a cultured pearl drop capped by marquise-shaped diamonds.

A five-strand graduated cultured pearl necklace. The bar clasp is set with step- and circular-cut diamonds.

Opposite
The Begum wearing a sari and some of her favourite pearl jewels, photographed at her villa, Yakymour, in the hills above Cannes in the South of France.

A ring with a cushion-shaped emerald in a double border of diamonds, with matching ear clips.

A gold compact by Robert Pouget. The lid, depicting the view from the Place de la Concorde up the Avenue des Champs-Élysées in Paris, is decorated with *calibré*-cut emeralds, rubies and diamonds.

Dating from the same period was a diamond necklace decorated with a profusion of marquise- and pear-shaped and brilliant- and step-cut diamonds (p. 247). It is probable that some of the stones for this came from a diamond fringe necklace (p. 245). To accompany the redesigned necklace, the Begum had a pair of pendent ear clips made in the form of a cascade with graduated pear- and marquise-shaped diamonds (p. 247). The twelve principle stones weighed a total of 46 cts and ranged from D (the most colourless and highest grade) to F on the diamond colour scale. When they were worn, the effect was dazzling. However, the most valuable piece, and the star lot of the sale, was a ring by Harry Winston, set with a step-cut diamond weighing 51.85 cts between tapered baguette diamond shoulders (p. 246). The diamond was D colour.

The Begum's collection included other less valuable but equally stylish jewels, such as the classic ring and matching ear clips set at the centre with a cushion-shaped emerald in a double border of brilliant-cut diamonds (left). She also owned a pair of ear clips of French manufacture set with a marquise-shaped emerald in a border of circular-cut rubies accented by floral clusters set with brilliant-cut diamonds (below).

The sale also featured a gold and gem-set compact by Robert Pouget, who was active in Paris in the mid-20th century (left). The lid, decorated with *calibré*-cut emeralds, rubies and diamonds, depicted the view from the Place de la Concorde up the Avenue des Champs Élysées; on the back was a map of the centre of Paris.

A pair of emerald, ruby and diamond ear clips.

A gold enamel and diamond compact by Cartier, Paris, *c.* 1930.

The Begum with Dame
Margot Fonteyn at the
Australian embassy in Paris
on 16 November 1965. The
reception followed a gala
performance by the Australian
Ballet of *Raymonda*, starring
Fonteyn and Rudolf Nureyev,
at the Théâtre des Champs
Élysées. The Begum is wearing
a diamond fringe necklace that
she later had redesigned and is
holding her gold and diamond
vanity case by Robert Pouget,
illustrated at right.

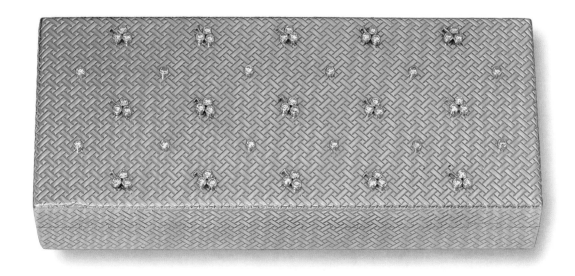

The Begum dancing with Prince Jacques, Duke of Orléans, at a gala in Paris on 1 July 1972. The Prince is transfixed by her diamond jewels.

A diamond ring by Harry Winston, set with a step-cut diamond weighing 51.85 cts between tapered baguette diamond shoulders.

A diamond necklace that the Begum commissioned in the late 1960s, probably using stones from her fringe necklace (p. 245). It is decorated with a profusion of pear- and marquise-shaped and brilliant- and step-cut diamonds. The pendent ear clips are designed as a cascade of pear- and marquise-shaped diamonds. The twelve principal pear-shaped diamonds have a total weight of 45.93 cts and range from 5.23 to 8.9 cts.

A cultured pearl and diamond
necklace, late 1960s. The front is
set with pear- and marquise-shaped
and brilliant-cut diamonds spaced
by yellow gold flowerheads set with
brilliant-cut diamonds, with a fringe of
fifteen cultured pearl drops capped by
marquise-shaped diamonds. The clasp
is similarly decorated.

Opposite
The Aga Khan and the Begum
photographed in the early 1950s. She
is wearing a gem-set Indian bangle.

The map was accented with diamonds. Robert Pouget also designed a gold vanity case in a basket-weave pattern set with diamonds in the form of clover leaves (p. 245). Inside were two compartments, a mirror, a lighter, a watch and a comb. Probably one of the few pieces recovered from the 1949 burglary was a Cartier gold and black enamel compact decorated with step-cut diamonds, from *c.* 1930 (p. 244).

In the Begum's last years she became infirm and was almost blind. Her one regret was that she had had no children of her own. However, she had enormous love and respect for the family of which she was a part for over fifty years. This was demonstrated by the instructions she left in her will that all the family jewelry should be returned to Prince Karim Aga Khan IV and his relations after her death, which accounts for the absence of the traditional Indian jewelry in the 2000 sale. Furthermore, except for certain bequests, she arranged that her estate should be left to the Aga Khan Foundation, which had been established by Prince Karim Aga Khan IV in 1967. It is a non-profit organization that concentrates on issues in health, education, rural development and the environment, and with strengthening civil society.

The Begum Om Habibeh died peacefully in France on 1 July 2000. She was buried next to her husband in the mausoleum on the banks of the Nile where she used to lay a red rose every day. ※

Nina Dyer

11

On 27 August 1957, an excited group of photographers and journalists gathered in the village of Collonge-Bellerive, on the shores of Lake Geneva, for the wedding of Prince Sadruddin Aga Khan and the beautiful Nina Dyer. The 24-year-old groom, whose home was the Château de Bellerive, was the second son of Sultan Muhammad Shah Aga Khan III, who had died the month before, and uncle of Prince Karim Aga Khan IV, 49th Imam of the Shia Ismaili Muslims. His bride was a renowned beauty of the time and a former model. Only 27, she had already been married and divorced from one of the richest men in Europe, Baron Hans Heinrich Thyssen-Bornemisza.

Very little is known about the elegant Nina Dyer and she is surrounded by an air of mystery. She is said to have been born in Kensington in London on 15 February 1930, the daughter of Stanley Dyer, owner of tea plantations in what was then Ceylon (Sri Lanka), and an Indian mother. She was brought up on the island, returning to England in her late teens, but soon moved to Paris, where she became a model for Balmain and Dior. It was not long before Nina began to frequent the highest circles of international society, particularly on the French Riviera, and by 1953 her exotic beauty had captured the interest of the 32-year-old Baron Thyssen-Bornemisza, whose grandfather had established a vast iron, steel and armaments conglomerate. He himself would later be famous as the owner of one of the world's great art collections. When he met Nina he was already married but this did not stop him from showering her with tokens of his love. Among his flamboyant early presents were the tiny inshore island of Pellew, in Jamaica, which was a Valentine's gift, and the valuable 'Blue Heart' diamond necklace by Van Cleef & Arpels (pp. 26, 28–31 and 252).

In June 1954, after divorcing his wife, the Baron married Nina. The engagement ring, by Harry Winston, was a marquise-shaped diamond of 27.22 cts set between tapered baguette diamond shoulders (p. 252). The diamond was D colour. Following the wedding, Nina continued to receive extraordinary examples of her husband's largesse: driving fast cars was one of her passions so he gave her two sports cars, for which Van Cleef & Arpels made solid gold keys. She was also fond of feline creatures and received at least one pet panther from 'Heini'. Her Siamese cat was the inspiration for a brooch designed by Christian Dior and made by Jean Claude Champagnat in yellow gold and *pavé*-set with fancy yellow diamonds. To accompany the brooch, Cartier created a pair of pendent earrings also in yellow gold and *pavé*-set with fancy yellow diamonds (p. 253).

After they were married, the couple continued to mix with members of the beau monde. Nina was always immaculately dressed and wore the beautiful jewels she received from her husband. The Van Cleef & Arpels archive reveals that in July 1954 the Baron brought in a step-cut sapphire of 56.43 cts, which they set in a ring decorated with pear-shaped baguette, navette and brilliant-cut diamonds. The firm also made a charming bird brooch using a cabochon ruby of 12 cts for its head and a cabochon sapphire of 56 cts for the body; both stones were supplied by the Baron.

Also dating from this period of Nina's life is a magnificent black pearl necklace, probably by Cartier, Paris. Natural black pearls are extremely rare and generally come from French Polynesia, particularly Tahiti, and the Pacific coasts of Panama and Mexico, where a particular kind of black-lipped oyster lives. Originally consisting of two strings, Nina's necklace was subsequently enlarged with another string of thirty pearls, which were rumoured to have come from Prince

The Van Cleef & Arpels pendant
given to Nina by the Baron
Thyssen-Bornemisza. The fancy
deep blue diamond of 30.62 cts,
known as the 'Blue Heart',
is suspended from a triangular
blue diamond of 3.81 cts and a
pear-shaped pink diamond of
2.05 cts in clusters of diamonds.

Baron and Baroness Thyssen-
Bornemisza at a charity ball at
the Monte Carlo Sporting Club
on 17 August 1954. Nina had
married the Baron two months
earlier on 23 June. She is wearing
her marquise-shaped diamond
engagement ring of 27.22 cts by
Harry Winston (illustrated above).

Page 250
A portrait of Nina Dyer by
Studio Harcourt, Paris, 1950s.

A pair of ear clips set with two
cushion-shaped sapphires of
17 and 14.20 cts respectively
in a cluster of navette and
pear-shaped diamonds.

Felix Yusupov's historic collection. However, the necklace that was later sold at auction boasted two strings of forty-nine pearls and one of fifty-three, which suggests that it must been further elongated at some point (p. 263). Each string could be detached from the clasp and worn separately.

Unfortunately, the marriage soon fell apart as the couple found they were incompatible; Nina told a journalist that her husband was 'obsessed with finance and high society' and he said she had a different sense of humour from his. As part of their divorce settlement in 1956, the Baron gave her a château in France and allowed her to keep most of the magnificent jewelry he had given her, as well as the Caribbean island.

After her divorce, Nina became involved with the charming and eligible bachelor Prince Sadruddin Aga Khan. His mother was Princess Andrée, the third wife of the Aga Khan III, and he was born in Neuilly-sur-Seine on 17 January 1933. He had been educated at Harvard and was on the brink of a distinguished career at the United Nations, where he was UN High Commissioner for Refugees, 1965–77. He also became a well-known philanthropist, in the family tradition. Prior to the couple's marriage, Nina converted to Islam.

Baron Thyssen-Bornemisza
introduces Nina, who was fond
of feline creatures, to a baby
leopard in Lugano in 1954.

A sapphire and diamond 'Great
Cat' clip brooch created by
Cartier for Nina in 1958. The
body of the panther is set with
circular-cut diamonds; the spots
are cabochon sapphires and
the eyes are marquise-shaped
emeralds. The paws and the
tail are articulated. The clip
could be attached to a five-
string graduated cultured pearl
necklace (opposite).

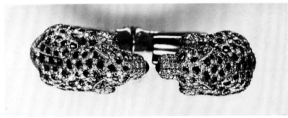

Archive photographs (above) of a bangle (right) by Cartier, Paris, created in 1958 to match the 'Great Cat' clip (p. 254). The design is of two panthers facing each other. The bodies are *pavé*-set with circular-cut diamonds and cabochon sapphire spots; the noses are made of onyx. A mechanism in the base enables the bangle to be opened.

She said that her new religion gave meaning to her life. As part of her conversion, she took the name 'Shirin', which means 'sweetness'.

The death of the Aga Khan on 11 July 1957 plunged the family into mourning, so the wedding on 27 August in Collonge-Bellerive was relatively modest and intimate with just twenty-nine guests. The Begum Om Habibeh was too upset at the loss of her husband to attend, but sent her warmest wishes to the couple. Those present included Princess Andrée; Aly Khan, Prince Sadruddin's half brother, and his fiancée, the model Bettina; Aly Khan's two sons, Karim (the new Aga Khan) and Amyn, and Yasmin, his daughter by Rita Hayworth. Pathé News filmed the guests arriving for the civil ceremony at the town hall (it was followed by a Muslim wedding at the château, conducted by two imams) and the commentary noted that the bride was wearing a pearl-grey organza dress by Christian Dior. The elegant outfit was augmented by a sapphire and diamond brooch with matching ear clips. Nina's engagement ring, made by Harry Winston, was set with a step-cut D colour diamond weighing 32.07 cts, mounted between tapered baguette diamond shoulders (p. 258).

In 1960, Cartier created a bangle of fluted yellow gold for Nina. The two panther heads at the terminals are mounted in platinum and set with circular-cut diamonds, cabochon sapphires and have emerald eyes. The bangle could also be used as the stylish handle of a suede bag (right). The two panther heads could be detached and worn as ear clips or attached to a gold and diamond frame created by Cartier for a brocade evening bag, as shown in the archive photograph above.

The wedding of Prince
Sadruddin Aga Khan and Nina
Dyer took place at Collonge-
Bellerive in Switzerland on
27 August 1957. Nina's step-cut
diamond engagement ring by
Harry Winston (right) can be seen
on her left hand as she signs the
register at the civil ceremony.
The diamond, weighing 32.07
cts, is mounted between tapered
baguette diamond shoulders.

The fact that Nina had married two millionaires in fairly quick succession brought her a certain notoriety. She remarked: 'People have called me a schemer, but nothing is further from the truth. Luck just comes my way without my doing anything about it.' Magnificient jewels also continued to come her way. One of the first presents she received from her new husband, in acknowledgment of her love of feline creatures, was a Cartier diamond and sapphire panther, mounted as a jabot pin (p. 264). The diamond clasp could be exchanged with a 30 cts sapphire set in a cluster of brilliant-cut diamonds. The panther, which was similar to one owned by the Duchess of Windsor (see p. 86), could also be removed from the pin and mounted on a large coral cabochon.

This was Nina's first Cartier 'Great Cat' jewel and others soon followed. In 1958, she acquired an articulated panther set with diamonds and sapphires that could be worn in different ways: as a brooch or as the clasp of a five-strand cultured-pearl necklace (pp. 254 and 255). Cartier also designed a bangle of two panthers facing each other, set with 1,142 circular diamonds and 331 cabochon sapphires (p. 256). The bangle could be opened by rotating the panthers. Two years later, in 1960, another panther bangle was added to Nina's

collection. This one was made of fluted yellow gold with the terminals formed by two panther heads, again in diamonds and sapphires, mounted in platinum. The heads could be unmounted and worn as ear clips, or used to decorate the gold frame of a brocade clutch bag. This versatile piece could also form an unusual handle for an evening bag (p. 257). In this period Cartier was known for creating bags with handles made of gold and gemstones. The Duchess of Windsor had one set with turquoises and rubies, and King Farouk of Egypt bought one with a yellow gold handle of diamond flowers for his fiancée. However, Nina's was probably the most flamboyant. A ring in the form of a recumbent leopard was a further addition to her Cartier 'Great Cat' set (p. 264).

However, jewelry was not the only lavish gift given to Nina by Prince Sadruddin. He bought her an eleven-acre property called Tiamo ('I love you' in Italian) opposite the island in Jamaica that Baron Thyssen-Bornemisza had bestowed on her. She was reputed to cross to the uninhabited island on bamboo rafts with friends for some discreet sunbathing. Sadly, the romantic name of the Caribbean estate soon became associated with the past; the couple separated in 1960 and divorced in 1962 on the grounds of incompatibility.

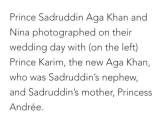

Prince Sadruddin Aga Khan and Nina photographed on their wedding day with (on the left) Prince Karim, the new Aga Khan, who was Sadruddin's nephew, and Sadruddin's mother, Princess Andrée.

An emerald and diamond clip brooch (top) set with a square step-cut emerald of 37.41 cts bordered by navette diamonds. It was created in 1960 by Cartier, Paris, for Prince Sadruddin Aga Khan. Harry Winston designed an emerald and diamond ring (above) to match the brooch.

Opposite
Emerald and diamond pendent ear clips, each one set with a hexagonal faceted emerald in a half border of navette diamonds. The briolette emerald pendent drops are capped by navette diamonds.

As with her divorce from Baron Thyssen-Bornemisza, Nina had a handsome settlement, said to be $1.4 million. In November of that year she consoled herself by ordering a Ferrari 250 GT California SWB Spyder, one of the world's most desirable cars. She also acquired another panther brooch from Cartier: the animal's head was carved in black jasper and had fancy yellow marquise-shaped diamond eyes (p. 253).

Although Nina had everything that life could provide in terms of luxury, the luck of which she had boasted began to run out. She suffered from depression and on 3 July 1965 her body was found by her Portuguese manservant in the bedroom of her apartment in Garches, in the Île-de-France west of Paris; next to her was a half-empty bottle of sleeping pills. She was only 35. Her fortune was left in trust for animal welfare.

Except for her striking looks, captured in photographs and on film, hardly anything is known about what kind of person Nina was, not least because she disappeared from the social scene at such a young age. Those who knew her best have also passed away: the Baron (who had three more wives) in 2002 and Prince Sadruddin (who married again in 1972) in 2003. One tangible legacy of this beautiful woman was her magnificent jewelry collection; several items from it were sold on 1 May 1969 at the first of Christie's 'Magnificent Jewelry' sales, held at the Hotel Richemond in Geneva.

One of the last pieces given to Nina by Sadruddin before their marriage broke up was an emerald and diamond clip brooch by Cartier, Paris. It consists of a square step-cut emerald of 37.41 cts set in a border of twenty navette diamonds weighing approximately 15 cts. To match the brooch, Harry Winston created a ring with a step-cut emerald of 16.38 cts, also in a border of navette diamonds (left). To complete the suite, Winston supplied a pair of emerald and diamond ear clips, each one composed of a hexagonal faceted emerald, weighing together 7.50 cts, in a half-border of navette diamonds from which was suspended a briolette emerald pendent drop capped by navette diamonds (p. 261). The two emerald drops weighed 26 cts.

The star lot at the sale was the three-strand black pearl necklace the Baron had given Nina. It is probably the most important black pearl necklace ever to be auctioned and was accompanied by a pair of black pearl and diamond ear clips by Cartier, Paris (p. 263). Each pearl is held in a spiral border of navette diamonds.

Opposite
Nina, wearing two strings of her
black pearl necklace, follows
the Begum Aga Khan and the
model Bettina, fiancée of Prince
Aly Khan, Prince Sadruddin's
half brother, down the steps at
Longchamp, 29 June 1958.

Nina's three-strand black pearl
necklace, probably by Cartier,
Paris, and considered the most
important black pearl necklace
ever to have been offered at
auction. The pearls measure
from 5.5 to almost 14 mm in
diameter. The colour is natural,

with variations from a greenish
hue to aubergine. Each string
could be detached and worn
separately. Nina's black pearl
ear clips (centre) are in a spiral
mount of graduated navette
diamonds, by Cartier, Paris.

Prince Sadruddin Aga Khan and Nina, photographed at Château de Bellerive, their home in Switzerland. She is wearing the jabot pin (below) designed by Cartier as a crouching panther and made of circular-cut diamonds and sapphires. The eyes are emeralds. The clasp at the base of the pin, which was composed of *pavé*-set circular-diamonds, could be exchanged with a sapphire of 30 cts in a cluster of brilliant-cut diamonds (as in the photograph). The panther could also be removed from the pin and mounted on a large red coral cabochon.

Archive photographs (above) from Cartier, Paris, of the ring (above left) created to match Nina's 'Great Cat' collection.

Prince Sadruddin Aga Khan and Nina Dyer photographed on 21 August 1957 in London on their way to Switzerland for their wedding. She is wearing one string of her black pearl necklace and a coral and diamond brooch (above) by Cartier, Paris. The rose is carved from an extremely rare coral of a deep-red colour known as Moor of Japan.

The diamond and sapphire 'Great Cat' jewels were another highlight of the sale, as well as a coral and diamond brooch in the form of a rose, also by Cartier, Paris (above).

Other lots included the two diamond engagement rings by Harry Winston (pp. 252 and 258), the Siamese cat brooch designed by Christian Dior (p. 253), and a pair of ear clips, each set with a cushion-shaped sapphire, of 17 and 14.20 cts respectively, in a cluster of navette and pear-shaped diamonds (p. 250).

Cartier had also supplied Nina with a gold compact featuring on its lid a leopard of platinum set with diamonds and sapphires surmounted by a princely crown. This, and an enamel and diamond lion brooch, as well as some minor pieces, were also in the 1969 sale.

The stunning pieces that were in Nina's collection are not only a testament to the sophisticated craftsmanship and creativity of the jewelers of the 1950s and 1960s but are also a tribute to the taste and elegance of the unfathomable Nina Dyer. ✳

Hélène Rochas

12

The story of the life of Hélène Rochas looks as if it came straight from the pages of a romantic novel by Barbara Cartland. The plot begins, 'one evening in 1941, in a Paris Metro station, a beautiful girl had a chance encounter with a stranger which would change the course of her life forever…'.

That night the beautiful girl was Nelly Brignole, 19 years old and studying acting. The stranger was Marcel Rochas, one of the most renowned French couturiers of his time, almost 20 years her senior. Her large aquamarine eyes and graceful posture, the product of years of classical ballet, totally mesmerized him. The following day she was invited to visit him at his atelier. This was the beginning of a great love story. He became her Pygmalion, shaping her into one of the most elegant women in Paris. She became his muse and the beautiful Nelly was transformed into Hélène. Less than two years later, in November 1942, he married her. They had one child already – François – and in 1944, a few months before the liberation of France, Sophie was born. In Hélène's honour Marcel launched the perfume 'Femme', one of his wedding gifts, and everything was created to enhance her beauty. Soon she became the image of La Maison Rochas, but Hélène was not only beautiful; thanks to Marcel's tuition she became a valued and supportive collaborator.

Marcel also found the perfect home for his family. They moved to number 40 Rue de Barbet de Jouy, in one of the most elegant areas of Paris. The apartment was on the ground floor of a 19th-century *hôtel particulier* with a lovely garden planted with only white flowers. To help in the decoration Marcel instructed Georges Geffroy, the most sought after interior decorator of his time, and together they created the elegant and sophisticated interior with important pieces from the First Empire, including the two gueridons that were once in the collection of the Murat family. In this sophisticated environment Hélène could flourish into the icon of beauty and elegance for which she would become renowned. In the years with Marcel she met the most fascinating personalities of the time, from Marie-Laure de Noailles to the British ambassador Alfred Duff Cooper and his legendary wife, Lady Diana.

Sadly this love story came to an end in 1955 with the premature death of Marcel Rochas at the age of 53. Hélène took over the company, closing the couture section and focussing on the perfumes, throwing herself into this new venture with great talent. She launched fragrances including Madame Rochas and Eau de Rochas, both great successes. A few years after her husband's death, she met the theatre impresario André Bernheim and they married in 1958. Unfortunately this relationship also came to an end, in 1965. Her interests extended from fashion to art and from design to music. In Paris she maintained the apartment at Rue de Barbet de Jouy, and in New York a pied-à-terre on Fifth Avenue decorated by François Catroux. Hélène was a respected figure of the *beau monde*, an extremely kind and gracious woman whose exquisite manners and taste in fashion made her the personification of Parisian elegance. She was admired by such friends as Yves Saint Laurent, Pierre Bergé and Guy de Rothschild. She was close friends with Maria Callas and was often invited to spend vacations with the singer and Aristotle Onassis on the yacht 'Christina'. Callas gave her a photograph of the star as Violetta from *La Traviata* with the dedication: 'To Hélène, si chère amie et si charmante personne si rare aujourd'hui. Maria 1968'. Hélène and Callas not only shared a sincere friendship but also an appreciation for beautiful Van Cleef & Arpels creations such as the delicate flower brooches for which

the firm was famous. Hélène's collection included a beautiful ruby and diamond 'magnolia' brooch, the petals invisibly set with tiny *calibré* rubies, the long detachable stem realized in baguette diamonds. To go with this brooch the French firm also created a pair of ear clips set with Burmese rubies in a double border of brilliant-cut diamonds.

In 1965 Hélène organized the My Fair Lady Ball, held at La Grande Cascade restaurant in Bois de Boulogne, Paris. That evening the glittering international set was there in force (see pages 92, 239). For the occasion Hélène was wearing a necklace designed as two lines of diamonds connected at the centre by a cluster of diamonds supporting a double loop. Van Cleef & Arpels used to lend such jewels from its collection to important clients for special occasions. The following year, Hélène hosted the Second Empire Ball for the centenary of the Casino Foundation in Monaco. The glamorous event was held in the beautiful Salle Garnier and the Casino Terraces of the Opéra de Monte-Carlo. Her beautiful turquoise, silk and black lace gown was enhanced by a magnificent set of turquoise and diamond jewels by Van Cleef & Arpels (p. 275). The great French firm took inspiration for the necklace design from the '*collier de la liberté*', an 18th-century emerald and diamond necklace donated by a French aristocratic lady to the American forces so that it could be sold and the money used in order to finance the American Revolutionary War against the British. In her hair she wore a brooch and matching ear clips, another creation by Van Cleef & Arpels from the 1960s. It is curious to note that both these necklaces were later borrowed by her friend Maria Callas; the diamond one to celebrate the birthday of Aristotle Onassis with his children; the turquoise one for a premiere in Paris.

In November 2013 at Christie's, Geneva, a selection of jewels from the collection of Hélène Rochas was presented at auction. These beautiful pieces gave a glimpse of Hélène's refinement of taste, not only in fashion but also in choosing her adornments: pieces bought less for the intrinsic value of the stones than for the quality of the design. This can be seen in a photograph of her taken by Baron in 1950 (opposite), which depicts a young and radiant Hélène wearing a gown designed for her by her husband Marcel; on her neck is a necklace in yellow gold and aquamarines, which echo and accentuate the vivid colour of her eyes.

A gold and aquamarine *parure* by René Boivin, 1950s. This kind of *parure* was created so that the necklace could be worn with or without the long pendant. Hélène Rochas (opposite), photographed by Baron *c.*1950, is modelling a dress designed by her husband and wearing the aquamarine *parure* by Boivin.

Previous page
Hélène Rochas photographed by André Ostier, *c.*1945; a mystery-set ruby and diamond 'magnolia' brooch, by Van Cleef & Arpels.

Above
Marcel and Hélène Rochas
with their children Sophie and
François, taken in 1951.

Opposite, top
A striking 'tiger' brooch by
René Boivin, late 1950s. The
flexible crouching tiger, set with
colourless and yellow stripes,
was designed to be worn on
the shoulder.

Opposite, below
Hélène Rochas wearing the
tiger brooch on her shoulder.

This outstanding piece of jewelry was created by Boivin – one of the most sought after creators of the 20th century (see pages 112, 117). The necklace can be worn in different ways, with or without a long pendant or with a centre clasp that can be removed and substituted. Other elegant pieces from the French firm included an elegant 'melon-slice bangle' in platinum and diamond from 1932. Another striking creation was the 'tiger' shoulder brooch, again from the 1950s: the body of the animal designed as platinum and colourless diamond stripes alternating with yellow-gold and yellow-diamond stripes. From the 1950s Hélène also had three yellow-gold, diamond, ruby and sapphire bracelets with a honeycomb motif popular in the late 1930s (p. 283). But probably her favourite Boivin creations were a pair of ear clips called 'Algues' from 1966, which appear frequently in photographs of Hélène taken over many years (p. 277).

Above
In May 1966, Hélène Rochas hosted the Second Empire Ball for the centenary of the Casino Foundation in Monaco. The glamorous event was held in the beautiful Salle Garnier and the Casino Terraces of the Opéra de Monte-Carlo. Here Hélène welcomes Her Highness the Begum Aga Khan III, who wears a diamond tiara.

Left
Hélène Rochas receives Gunter Sachs, who is dressed as a Russian prince, at the Second Empire Ball.

Right
Hélène welcomes Prince Rainier III of Monaco and Princess Grace to the ball.

Bottom
Prince Rainier III of Monaco (seated, right) and Princess Grace relaxing with other guests during the ball. Princess Grace, like her host Hélène Rochas, wears a *parure* of sapphires and diamonds, created by Van Cleef & Arpels, and an historic diamond tiara from the Napoleonic period, from the Van Cleef & Arpels collection.

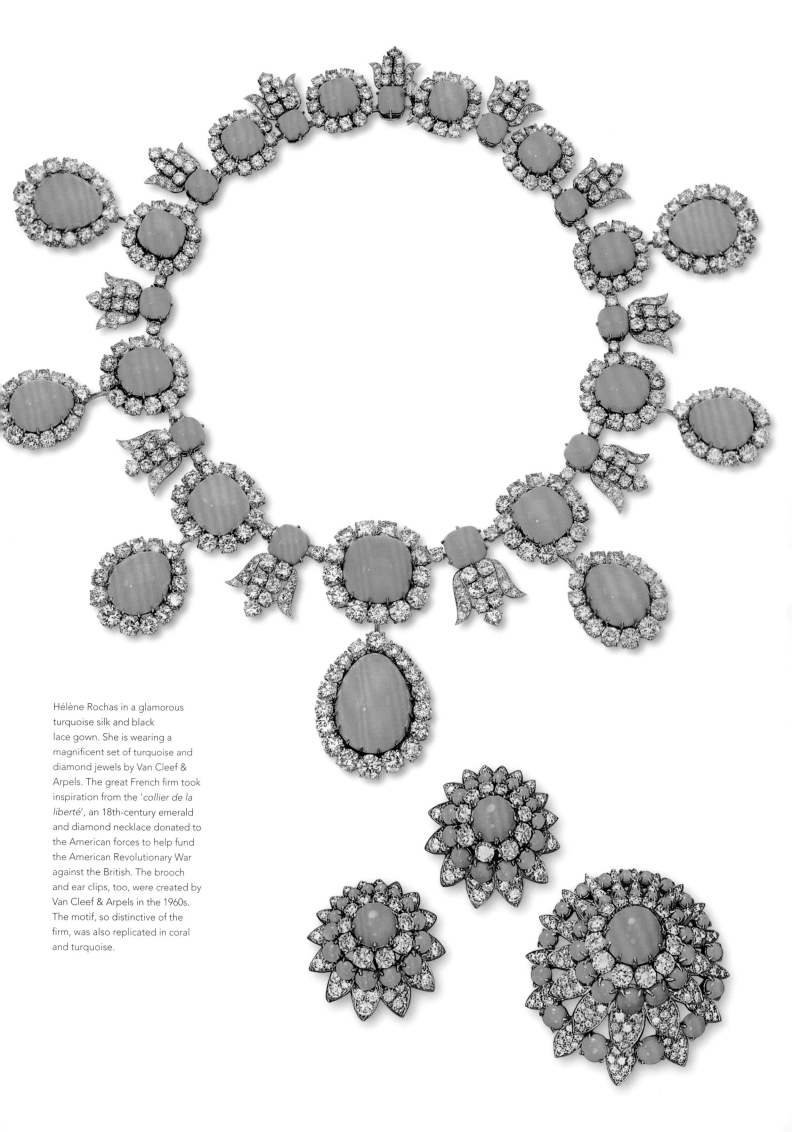

Hélène Rochas in a glamorous turquoise silk and black lace gown. She is wearing a magnificent set of turquoise and diamond jewels by Van Cleef & Arpels. The great French firm took inspiration from the '*collier de la liberté*', an 18th-century emerald and diamond necklace donated to the American forces to help fund the American Revolutionary War against the British. The brooch and ear clips, too, were created by Van Cleef & Arpels in the 1960s. The motif, so distinctive of the firm, was also replicated in coral and turquoise.

Right
A photograph from the early
1960s of (from left) Hélène
Rochas, the shipping tycoon
Aristotle Onassis, Maria Callas
and Kim d'Estainville.

Below
An elegant vanity case by Cartier
c. 1920. The lid is decorated
with black enamel in a floral
pattern enhanced with diamond
collets, with an onyx handle as
a push piece.

Left and below
Hélène Rochas was a great friend
and admirer of Maria Callas.
Here they are photographed
together at the Théâtre des
Champs Elysées in December
1968. Hélène wears her favourite
black and white pearl and
diamond 'Algues' ear clips by
René Boivin, *c.* 1966 (pictured
below). Callas is wearing her
ruby and diamond ear clips.

Bottom
Another Boivin creation, from the
1930s: a platinum and diamond-
tranche 'melon-slice bangle'.

Each of the 'Algues' ear clips was set with a grey or white cultured pearl surmounted by platinum- and diamond-set leaves. She also owned a pendant designed as an articulated yellow-gold, peridot and moonstone fish, created around 1971.

Hélène not only admired contemporary creations but also loved delicate and rare period jewelry, such as the exquisite Cartier pendant necklet, designed as a plaque of rock crystal engraved with floral motifs, set in platinum and diamonds on a black silk cord: a beautiful example of Cartier's creativity from 1912. Hélène wore this pendant to great effect on a velvet black gown decorated with white camellias, on the occasion of the Proust Ball hosted by Baron and Baroness Guy de Rothschild in 1972 at Château de Ferrières. Another piece she had from Cartier was an elegant vanity case in yellow gold, black enamel, diamond and onyx from the 1920s.

Cartier also created for her an exquisite choker in faceted aquamarine beads, the clasp formed by a cushion-shaped kunzite of over 60 cts set in the centre of a border designed as a *pavé*-set diamond torsade. This choker was created to go with a stunning diamond bangle, a creation from 1968 by Fulco di Verdura, the hinged bangle designed as a diamond torsade band, the terminals decorated with a cushion-shaped aquamarine of 22.91 cts and a cushion-shaped pink topaz of 28.17 cts. Hélène also loved to wear long necklaces: in gold with hanging charms; long strings of white and black freshwater pearls; or more elaborate designs such as a string of cultured pearls

alternated with lapis lazuli hoops and large white gold beads set with diamonds and sapphires, or with sapphires and turquoises. However, the most unusual example is one composed of small onyx beads, joined together by a motif composed of two elements of engraved coral and diamonds culminating in an onyx bead tassel. The side is decorated by a coral sculpted in the shape of a rose, the petals trimmed by diamonds. This is probably a brooch by Cartier from the 1950s that was already in Hélène's collection. Later she must have asked the French firm to incorporate it in this elegant necklace. Cartier also created a pair of onyx, coral and diamond ear clips to match this piece.

At the beginning of the 1970s 'La Belle Hélène', as she was known, started a relationship with an elegant French aristocrat, Kim d'Estainville, who had been a correspondent for *Paris Match*, owned of a number of fashion boutiques and, together with Pierre Bergé,

A long necklace of onyx beads with a coral and diamond brooch designed as a rose. The strings of beads are joined together at the ends by two elements of diamond and engraved coral, forming a tassel at the front. The rose must originally have been a Cartier brooch from the 1950s, later used to create this elegant necklace, probably also by this legendary French firm.

Below
A pair of Cartier diamond, coral and onyx ear clips designed to accompany the necklace.

Opposite
Hélène Rochas, and Baron Alexis de Redé, at the Paris Opera for an evening in memory of director Luchino Visconti. She is welcomed by Baron Guy de Rothschild, 1980.

Above
A Cartier creation: a torsade choker of faceted aquamarine beads, the diamond clasp set at the centre with a cushion-shaped kunzite of over 60 cts.

Right
A creation from 1968 by Fulco di Verdura, the hinged bangle designed as a diamond torsade band, the terminals decorated with a cushion-shaped aquamarine of 22.91 cts and a cushion-shaped pink topaz of 28.17 cts, *c.1968*.

Opposite
Hélène Rochas photographed at the Paris Opera for the premiere of Francis Ford Coppola's *The Godfather*. She is wearing her Boivin pearl and diamond ear clips and her rare rock-crystal, diamond and black enamel *sautoir* by Jean Fouquet, *c.1924*.

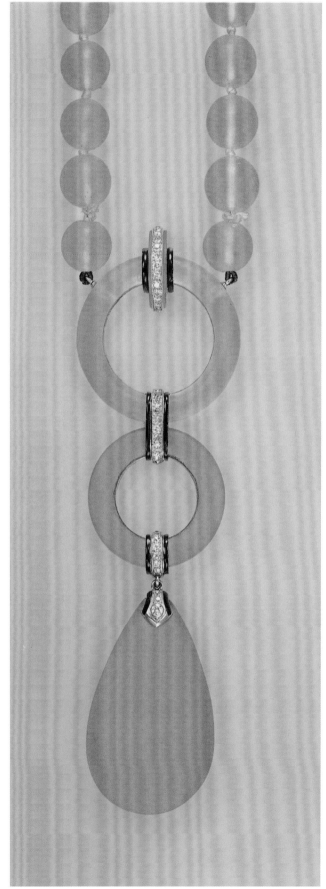

co-produced the play *Equus* in France. This was the start of a new chapter in her life. In 1970, Hélène, together with her two children François and Sophie, agreed to sell their 80 per cent share of the Rochas perfume brand for $40m. Following this, Hélène and Kim lived together and enjoyed a whirl of social events and parties, sharing their time between apartments in Paris and New York. They spent their summer vacations at Kim's villa on the Côte d'Azur or on her 115ft yacht. They both shared a passion for art and he was responsible for channelling Hélène's great sense of style and curiosity in the direction of a form of art which was out of fashion in that period – Art Deco.

Hélène soon started to collect Art Deco paintings and furniture, and this new passion also resulted in the acquisition of two beautiful jewels from La Maison Fouquet, one of the leading Parisian jewelers. Georges Fouquet was the son of Alphonse, who founded the firm in 1860. Alphonse was an artisan known and respected for his meticulously chased and enamelled creations in the Neo-Renaissance style, but Georges emerged during the Art Nouveau movement together with such master goldsmiths as the great René Lalique. From the 1890s he embraced the new artistic styles and technical possibilities of the era to superb effect.

Hélène Rochas photographed around 1970, wearing a ruby and diamond camellia brooch by Van Cleef & Arpels; a pair of cluster ear clips in rubies and diamonds, again by Van Cleef & Arpels (below); and two 'honeycomb' bracelets by Boivin, one set with diamonds and one with rubies (opposite, below).

Right
Hélène in the late 1960s, wearing
a brooch by Nardi of Venice
designed as a beetle (below).
The body is made from pink
coral and the wings are carved
jadeite plaques, all bordered
with diamonds.

Below
The full set of three gold
'honeycomb' bracelets from
the 1950s: one with diamonds,
one with rubies, and one with
sapphires.

Georges Fouquet also opened one of the most famous shops in Paris during that period. The place chosen was 6 Rue Royale, and both the interior and exterior were decorated in spectacular style by Alphonse Mucha, famously the creator of publicity posters for the great actress Sarah Bernhardt. Mucha also designed Bernhardt a spectacular hand ornament consisting of a bangle and ring joined together. This jewel, designed and executed in 1899, is considered one of the most important of the Art Nouveau period. The bangle is a coiled serpent, its head decorated with a mosaic of opals. The ring matches the bangle and they are joined together by a fine double chain. In 1919 Jean Fouquet, Georges's son, joined his father as a jewelry designer.

Jean's name appeared as a designer for the Exposition des Arts Décoratifs in 1925 and was represented in all subsequent exhibitions. He would create jewels with rigorous geometric shapes and contrasting colours, such as bangles with dramatic and bold designs on a large scale and long necklaces in opaque rock crystal with large pendants.

Following suggestions from Kim and Hélène's interior decorator, François Catroux, she redecorated her apartment at Rue de Barbet de Jouy. Now the beautiful 18th-century and First Empire furniture was set in a more contemporary scheme, mixed with paintings by Wassily Kandinsky, dated June 1925, and Ben Nicholson, dated 1933. The lighting created a more intriguing ambience thanks to the stunning 'cobra' lamps by Edgar Brandt et Daum (c. 1925) and the 'candelabre deux serpents' from Edouard Marcel Sandoz (c. 1931) masterfully displayed next to a screen by Jean Dunand called 'Les Cygnes' ('The Swans'; c. 1935). Hélène's music room was decorated with standard lamps and armchairs by Diego and Alberto Giacometti. The four portraits she commissioned from Andy Warhol in 1970 had a strong impact on this new arrangement. In the 1980s her relationship with Kim d'Estainville came to an end, but Hélène remained a prominent social figure and patron of the arts.

The 1980s also saw her invited to rejoin the family firm by the president of Rochas, Jacques Pecqueriaux; he declared her to be 'our nose, our intuition, our mirror'. Hélène continued to attend all the important social events of her milieu and to collect the latest fashions. These included two pieces from Marina B, a granddaughter of Sotirio Bulgari who left the family firm to become a prestigious jeweler in her own right: in 1986 a pair of yellow-gold, diamond, cabochon sapphire, ruby and emerald pendent earclips; in 1988 a pair with a geometric design in baguette and brilliant-cut diamonds mounted in white gold. On 6 August 2011, Hélène passed away peacefully in the house she loved so much, which had been her home in Paris for over sixty years. She will always be remembered as a discreet and gracious lady, and her beauty and taste remain as celebrated as her fairy-tale life. Christie's auctioned her collection in Paris on 27 September 2012. The catalogue was a tribute to her great sense of style, and its beautiful photographs allow us a glimpse into the world of this unforgettable lady. ✖

Opposite
Hélène Rochas photographed in 1987 in her music room. She is wearing one of her last acquisitions: an elegant pair of pendent ear clips called 'Francesca', by Marina B, in diamond, cabochon sapphire, ruby and emerald, created in 1986 (above).

An elegant creation by Jean Fouquet, son of Georges, from the late 1920s: a rare yellow-gold cuff bangle designed with a spherical motif in relief.

Ganna Walska

13

Ganna Walska cuts a striking figure even among the fashionable women presented in this volume. Her style and the jewels she wore were as inimitable as the lady herself. 'Because I am not dressed as Number 2768 of Schiaparelli, Mainbocher's "Wally Blue" or Molyneux's Spring Model 1938, people may call me eccentric when I am only original in the true meaning of the word', declared Ganna in the memoir she wrote after moving to America at the start of the Second World War.

When her jewelry collection came up for auction in New York in 1971, the press described the collection as 'exotic and wonderfully designed' and 'including many fine gem-stones and a selection of Indian jewelry'. The sale total of $916,000 for 146 lots created a sensation in the midst of a recession and was at least double what had been expected. This sale, however, took place at a time when jewelry cataloguing was brief and little emphasis was placed on researching the origins of the pieces. As such, the remarkable true importance of this collection was not apparent. Discovering the origins of these jewels has been as intriguing as uncovering the true history of their owner.

Dedicating it to 'all those who are always seeking their place in the sun', Ganna Walska published her autobiography *Always Room at the Top* in 1943. In the opening chapter she professes that her main reason for writing her memoirs was that her 'secretive nature desired a confidant'. Secretive is an apt word, for in the first few chapters she refers obliquely to her youth spent in Poland and Russia, and writes that she travelled to the United States in her late teens. Her whole life story, in fact, seems dotted with discrepancies. One thing she is perfectly clear about is that her name was her own creation. Requiring a stage name for her chosen career as an opera singer, she tells us that like all Poles she loves dancing, especially the Waltz. 'So suddenly I said "Waltz, Valse, Walska…!"' And so, as Ganna Walska, she became a well-known, though somewhat unsuccessful, opera and concert singer in America and Europe from the 1920s through to the 1940s, and led an interesting and extravagant life.

Accounts of her origins vary. According to one operatic biography she was born in Belleville, Arkansas, in 1885. Another reputable, and possibly more accurate publication reports that she was born on 26 June 1887 in Poland, daughter of Napoleon and Karolina Puacz. Ganna maintains that she was educated in Warsaw and that by the age of 17 was married to Baron Arcadie d'Eingorne and living in St Petersburg. Shortly after their marriage, her husband contracted tuberculosis and in the hope of finding a cure they spent three years in a Swiss clinic where he eventually died. By all accounts, by 1915 she was in New York, beautiful and with a consuming desire to be a great singer.

Ganna's singing career started out with a series of concerts; on 18 February 1918 she made her debut in a recital with Caruso at the Biltmore Morning Musicals, singing an aria from *Pagliacci* and a duet from *The Pearl Fishers* with the famous tenor himself. Two years later she was signed up to sing with the Chicago Opera Company in their 1921 season. She had also met the man who would play such an important role in her life, Harold McCormick, the millionaire son of the so-called Chicago Reaper King, himself the chairman of the International Harvester Company, and, of obvious importance to Ganna, an 'angel' for the Chicago Opera Company. During this period she had embarked on the second of her six marriages, this time to Dr Joseph Fraenkel, a neurologist many years her senior. By 1936, the United Press Association reported that she was 'estimated to have married fortunes totalling $125,000,000 in her marital ventures with four wealthy men. She likewise was believed to have spent one-twelfth of this sum in attempting to further her great ambition to become an opera star.' What proportion of this fabulous wealth she spent on her jewelry collection was not guessed at, but it must have been extensive.

The earliest surviving photographs of Ganna Walska show her wearing simple pearl jewelry: it was not until the early 1920s that her great passion for acquiring and wearing spectacular jewels emerged. Her time with Dr Fraenkel was brief, for he died within a few years of their marriage. Shortly after his death, friends persuaded her to join them on a trip to Paris, and during the long voyage across the Atlantic she met Harold McCormick again, who introduced her to a fellow passenger, Alexander Smith Cochran. Cochran was swiftly smitten by the ravishing Ganna; even before the voyage was completed he had proposed to her. According to her memoir, Alec Cochran 'forcibly placed a perfect oriental pearl ring' on her finger saying, 'if by January you still do not want to marry me, send back this ring. I will understand that Harold McCormick is too much on your mind'. Ganna was hesitant to accept his offer of marriage but after many protestations she finally agreed, kept the ring, and married him in Paris in September 1920.

Alec Cochran was reputed to be the richest bachelor in the world and his wedding present to her was 'to go with Carte blanche to Cartier and choose anything' she desired. Her choice has never been revealed but it may well have been the fantastic yellow pear-shaped briolette diamond weighing 96.62 cts that was sold in 1971. This gem was originally mounted in a *sautoir*, so fashionable at that period, hanging from a chain of alternating platinum and diamond, and a rock crystal lynx. By the time it was auctioned it was capped by five small marquise diamonds and mounted with a simple tongue-piece fitting, by which it could be attached to a suitable necklace as a pendant. A few days after their marriage the Cochrans returned to America.

Ganna was determined to pursue her career in opera and initially Alec agreed to her wishes. Soon after their arrival in the United States, however, his attitude changed and he made it impossible for her to continue with her commitments to the Chicago Opera Company. Inevitably, their relationship started to

unravel. That Christmas, when they were in their New York house, Alec repeatedly asked Ganna what she wanted as a present and she would emphatically reply that she did not want anything.

Throughout her life Ganna was very interested in fashion, although she was not always ready to follow its dictates. She had her own sense of style, which often preceded the current vogues. A few weeks prior to Christmas she had visited Cartier in New York and decided to try on several bracelets to verify whether she 'would care to follow the trend of fashion', sometimes referred to rather unkindly as 'service stripes'. Ganna decided that she did not want to cover the 'natural beauty' of her wrists with the 'artificial beauty' of precious stones. Alec Cochran had spotted his wife at Cartier and returned there a few days later as he had 'almost half an hour to waste before luncheon' and if he bought some jewels for Ganna 'it would kill a few minutes' of his time. He had then unceremoniously thrust the package containing the jewels on her desk, which ensured that Ganna was enraged by the manner in which the gift was both chosen and given. She could not even bring herself to thank him. The present in question was a heart-shaped diamond ring of 21.15 cts (p. 309). This magnificent jewel, as well as the yellow-diamond briolette, was bought in the sale of 1971 by Van Cleef & Arpels, who renamed them the 'Walska Heart' and the 'Walska Briolette'.

Two weeks later, the couple returned to Paris, but Alec immediately left for England to indulge his passion for hunting. Despite an eventual reunion at their new home in Rue de Lübeck, the relationship gradually deteriorated; Ganna bitterly resented him for hindering her singing career and Alec became increasingly suspicious of her affections. They were divorced in July 1922 and within fourteen days she was married in Salzburg to Harold McCormick – also recently divorced, from the famous heiress Edith Rockefeller. Ganna's latest marriage was greeted by the French press with the suggestion that she had started a new fashion: 'two weeks of mourning after the final divorce decree!'

McCormick now set about trying to advance his wife's career while showering her with the wonderful jewels she adored. Sadly for Ganna, even his enormous wealth could not assure her of success on the opera stage and she received many negative reviews for her performances. It could, however, buy her the most

The 'Walska Briolette', a fancy vivid-yellow 96.62-ct diamond briolette from Cartier, Paris.

Left
Ganna Walska around 1914.

Page 288, above
Ganna Walska photographed around 1919, wearing a head ornament and her favourite pearls. The pearl and diamond pendant she wore would be included in the 1971 sale as Lot 40. The natural pearls measured 14 x 19 mm.

Page 288, below
A beautiful butterfly brooch by Boucheron (*c.* 1894); the body is a cushion-shaped Burmese ruby. The wings, formed by portrait-cut diamonds engraved by Bordinckx, are mounted *'en tremblant'*.

incredible jewels. In 1923 she acquired two fabulous necklaces from Cartier in Paris, which rank among the greatest pieces ever created by these jewelers. One was a sapphire and emerald necklace designed as a row of sapphire beads connected by sections of smaller emerald beads, from which hung a spectacular Mughal engraved emerald of 256.60 cts, carved with flowers and foliage, suspended from an engraved sapphire of 39.14 cts.

Cartier made many alterations to the necklace, which Hans Nadelhoffer refers to as 'chameleon-like' in his history of Maison Cartier. The first was undertaken in 1927, when the sapphire became a vase embellished with a diamond rim and handles, which was surmounted by an emerald of 33.58 cts engraved with leaves (the giardinetto motif was highly fashionable at this period, as was the combination of green and blue). This was then connected to the emerald and sapphire beads by two pear-shaped motifs *pavé*-set with onyx points and diamonds (p. 293). The next transformation was the addition of an important antique 'Russian' sapphire, rectangular-shaped, faceted and weighing 197.75 cts. The sapphire appears in the catalogue of Russia's Treasure of Diamonds and Precious Stones printed in Moscow in 1926 under the general supervision of Professor A. E. Fersman, a member of the Academy of Science of Russia. In the description of 'two beautiful brooches/fermoirs decorated with ancient sapphires from Ceylon', this sapphire mounted within a border of diamonds is described as a 'large sapphire of flat Hindu cutting... the setting is modern by Fabergé.' As this brooch was not included in the famous sale of treasures from the Russian State Jewels held in London in 1927, exactly how it was acquired by Cartier is unknown but in their archives it is simply referred to as the sapphire 'historique' from the Russian Tsars. In Ganna's necklace this sapphire was capped by diamonds and incorporated into the side of the necklace between the sapphire and emerald beads (pp. 294, 295). A few months later the 'Russian' sapphire became the pendent drop connected by an emerald rondel. Ganna's quest for perfection saw several further alterations; in the version from 1929 the smaller carved emerald and sapphire were removed and the 'Russian' sapphire surmounted the magnificent Mughal emerald drop (p. 297). This was one of the jewels she wore at the famous society wedding of Barbara Hutton to Prince Mdivani in Paris in 1933.

When the necklace appeared in the 1971 sale it was in yet another entirely different style, dating from the 1940s. The 'Russian' sapphire was the centre of the necklace, the sides composed of thirty sapphire beads from the original necklace, which were now divided by diamond-set spacers; the back was designed as a chain of diamonds on a sapphire bead clasp (p. 297). The Mughal emerald was sold separately as a pendant and the emerald rondel had become the centre of a sapphire, emerald and diamond pendant. In 1992, the 'Russian' sapphire appeared once again in the saleroom in Geneva. On this occasion it was the centre of a contemporary emerald bead torsade, supporting an emerald briolette drop.

The other marvellous necklace she bought from Cartier in 1923 was set with emeralds and diamonds.

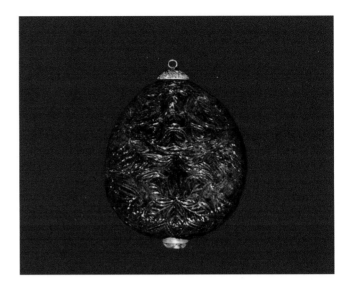

The front was elegantly fringed by a pendant of seven drop-shaped emerald beads weighing 167.54 cts in total, capped by diamonds and connected by lunette-shaped diamonds and two pear-shaped diamond scroll motifs. This was connected to a two-row emerald bead neckchain by a row of cabochon emeralds, the whole chain interspersed by variously cut diamonds. Again this necklace was obviously subject to many alterations, and by the time of her 1971 sale it had been totally dismounted. The only jewel surviving as a reminder of the former creation was a spectacular brooch, which was set with all the baguette and fancy-shaped diamonds, together with the scroll motifs formerly in the necklace. The fate of the emerald beads and drops is unknown.

In 1929 Ganna was one of several society ladies to add a Cartier chimera bangle to her collection. This bangle, designed by Charles Jacqueau, was set with two coral serpent's heads carved by the lapidary Dalvy; they were decorated with carved sapphire leaves and cabochon sapphires, and with diamond eyes and teeth.

Top
A carved Mughal emerald drop weighing 256 cts, originally from the Cartier sapphire, emerald and diamond necklace created in 1923.

Opposite
Between the time it was first created in 1923 and its final version in 1929, the wonderful Cartier emerald, sapphire and diamond necklace underwent several alterations. This original archive photograph from Cartier, Paris, shows the first rearrangement of 1927.

Left
Ganna Walska in fancy dress wearing her emerald, sapphire and diamond necklace by Cartier, Paris, in its second version of 1927, including the 'Russian' sapphire on one side.

Above
The 'Russian' sapphire in its original diamond mount as a brooch by Fabergé.

Opposite
This 1927 version can also be worn with the lateral sapphire briolette replaced by the chain of beads shown to one side.

Held between the serpents' jaws were two large, fluted emerald beads of 48.43 cts, and the back was decorated with blue and green enamel (p. 302). The bracelet was made as stock for Cartier in 1928 by Lavabre, and Ganna bought it the following July. In the 1971 sale it was described as an 'Indian Tawiz Arm Amulet'. Indeed, though made in France, the carved heads represented Makara, the mythical Indian sea serpent. The previous lot in her sale was similarly described, but was also a European interpretation of these exotic jewels. This sensational bangle, made by Van Cleef & Arpels in the late 1920s, was set with carved coral chimera heads decorated with sapphires and diamonds and holding jade beads between their jaws. The back of the bangle was decorated with green, blue and white enamel.

These two bangles are superb examples of Art Deco jewelry, which used a dramatic combination of colours, materials and symbolism. Another bangle in Ganna Walska's collection from a similar period was a version in onyx, carved emerald and diamond, almost certainly by Cartier. The hinged mount of platinum and onyx was decorated with brilliant-cut diamonds and the terminals were set with two large carved emerald beads.

In the late 1920s Ganna bought a wonderful coral and onyx fuchsia necklace from Cartier, originally designed as stock in 1925. The 1971 sale catalogue refers to a carved coral, carved emerald, onyx and pearl pendant necklace, which would fit the fuchsia jewel (for which the original drawings survive). Unfortunately the catalogue contains no photographs to confirm this.

Opposite
The diamond and black-enamel
pendant set with an historic
'Russian' sapphire can also be
worn in a diamond, emerald and
sapphire *sautoir*, as illustrated on
the opposite page. These can be
substituted by another pendant
set with two engraved emeralds
in a border of black enamel and
a ground of *pavé*-set diamonds,
itself bordered by *calibré*-cut
sapphires and supporting a
diamond fringe.

Above
The Mughal emerald and Russian
sapphire hang together from a
chain of emeralds and sapphires.

Below
The vastly altered necklace as it
appeared in the 1971 auction.

Above
A photograph from the Cartier
archives of an emerald and
diamond long necklace that
Walska bought from Cartier,
Paris in 1923.

Opposite, above
Ganna Walska photographed
by Baron de Meyer in the 1920s.
She is wearing the emerald
and diamond necklace created
by Cartier, Paris, in 1923 and a
matching pair of emerald and
diamond pendent earrings.
Other jewels are her emerald
and diamond clasp worn as a
bracelet centre and her heart-
shaped diamond ring. From
Ganna Walska, *Always Room
at the Top*, New York, 1943.

Opposite, below
This diamond brooch, which was
included in the 1971 auction,
appeared to be all that remained
from the original emerald drop
and diamond necklace that
Cartier had created in 1923.
The brooch was a cluster of
scroll motifs and the curiously
cut and shaped diamonds that
had originally formed integral
parts of the necklace. Sotheby's,
New York (Parke-Bernet).

The sale featured several other coral jewels of similar date and Art Deco influence, some signed by Cartier. These included a small group of hair ornaments and hatpins, the most interesting of which was in the form of a Japanese pagoda set with lapis lazuli, diamonds, carved jade and a cabochon sapphire. The design and materials were typical of Cartier's oriental style of the late 1920s. Other jewels included coral necklaces, some carved, some matched with jade, coral bracelets, and a stylish coral, diamond and black enamel ring. Also of note were the carved coral, carved emerald and pearl pendent ear clips, a brooch set with similar gemstones, and a carved jade of giardinetto form.

In 1929 Ganna bought a most unusual Cartier jewel, which the 1971 catalogue described simply as a 'crystal and diamond bracelet'. The most popular style of bracelets in the 1920s was a flat strap form, from which this was a complete departure. Of tubular form, it was composed of a flexible row of carved crystal demi-lune discs strung together on wire, the sides of each crystal set with brilliant-cut diamonds. The back was set with several platinum bars to strengthen the form of the jewel. Ganna's bracelet was the first that Cartier created in this style. The following year they made two further versions, one of which was sold to the actress Gloria Swanson and the second to Madame Coty, first lady of France.

In 1929, Ganna also acquired from Cartier a wonderful amethyst and diamond *sautoir* designed as a long rope of larger step-cut amethysts, alternating with pairs of smaller rectangular amethysts and with a large clasp of pear- and similarly shaped stones bordered by diamonds. *Sautoirs* were still highly fashionable at this period, but by 1936 Ganna needed an updated version.

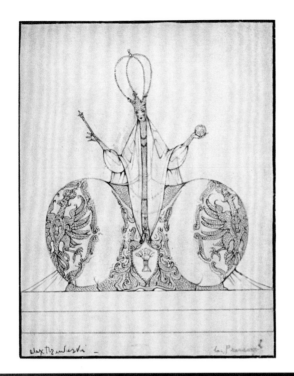

Cartier remounted most of the stones from this jewel and added a few to create a stylish fringed necklace and a pair of bracelets.

For the first few years of their marriage Harold McCormick is said to have spent a fortune attempting to promote her operatic career, but according to the critics she did not have the talent to succeed. Despite her husband's advice to relinquish her ambitions, Ganna travelled throughout America and Europe pursuing her quest. By 1929 she had left Chicago for Paris, agreeing to a separation from Harold. Once back in France she bought the Château de Galluis, halfway between Paris and Chartres, where she entertained the rich and famous with extravagant galas. She also spent time at the Théâtre des Champs-Elysées, which she had acquired out of her own funds in 1922, and where she organized various operatic events.

In 1931, the year Harold McCormick finally divorced her on the grounds of desertion, she made several major purchases from Cartier. In the early autumn she bought a wonderful carved ruby and diamond necklace designed as two rows of ruby beads with baguette diamond spacers; the front supported a fringe of fourteen rubies carved in the form of leaves and decorated with baguette and brilliant-cut diamonds. Of Indian inspiration, this necklace was one of the highly popular 'Tutti Frutti' jewels in the Cartier repertoire. In the same month she also purchased from them an extraordinary belt composed of fifteen carved jade circular plaques, each set with a cabochon ruby and with two larger carved jade and ruby plaques mounted as the clasp. The belt measured over 28 inches and there were two extra links to increase the size. The belt was accompanied by a pair of matching bracelets set with jade beads and jade and ruby plaques, one embellished with diamonds. Ganna had admitted to 'liking big jewels', and was 'fortunate enough to get them of any existing size and colour; twenty years before the actual fashion for big gems I designed for myself huge necklaces, bracelets and rings, and to make them I got the biggest stones I could find on the market, the largest generous Nature created.' These particular pieces were in fact stock designs from Cartier rather than designed by Ganna, but they were certainly big.

That November, Cartier had added to their stock a diamond necklace of Indian inspiration set with ten large triangular rose diamonds. Each stone was set in a border of brilliant-cut diamonds with the largest six hanging as a fringe at the front; they were connected by baguette diamonds and mounted on a back chain of marquise-shaped stones and smaller rose- and brilliant-cut diamond clusters (p. 306). Whether or not Ganna bought it that year is unclear, but in the 1971 sale it was presented in a completely altered style: the ten larger rose diamonds were still in brilliant-cut diamond borders, but now arranged as a fringe of five two-stone pendants supported by a chain of brilliant-cut diamonds; it was accompanied by a clip and a pair of pendent earrings set with similar stones (p. 307).

Left
A late 18th-century enamelled gold cuff from Jaipur, Rajastan, the form simulating a series of joined bangles, all set with rubies, emeralds and diamonds. The bands are also enamelled on the inside.

Opposite, top
An enamel, carved coral, sapphire, jade and diamond chimera bangle by Van Cleef & Arpels, 1920s.

Opposite, centre
A 1923 Cartier chimera bangle, with carved coral sea monsters, holding in their mouths two fluted cabochon emeralds weighing 48.43 cts. The back is decorated with green and blue enamel.

Above
An emerald, ruby and rose-diamond necklace from Madras, South India. This style of Indian necklace was usually worn by traditional dancers.

Opposite, top
A head ornament with an Indian motif, from Cartier, Paris. The decoration and materials evoke the antique Indian bracelet shown below.

Opposite, bottom
Champa-Kali ruby, diamond and gold cluster bracelet from India, dating to around 1800.

Right
Ganna Walska wearing a selection of Cartier jewels from her collection, including a 1930s head ornament similar in shape to the Cartier creation opposite.

Though Ganna Walska bought an enormous number of jewels from Cartier between the 1920s and the 1940s, the catalogue for her 1971 sale acknowledged only a small percentage of them as Cartier commissions or from Cartier stock. Indeed Van Cleef & Arpels received no mention at all, even though she was one of their most important patrons. The Paris firm of Chaumet is also known to have sold her several jewels including a sapphire of 67.34 cts in 1926. Surprisingly, the only piece in her sale recognized as being by Chaumet was a gold, ruby, emerald and diamond pendant necklace of typical 1940s style. The front was of gold scrolled openwork, the stylized buckle design set with two large carved rubies, two pear-shaped and oval rubies, and cylindrical-shaped emeralds; it was decorated with rose- and brilliant-cut diamonds on a necklace of flexible 'gas-pipe' linking. As with so many of Ganna's jewels, the necklace had been subject to alterations and it was sold with a pendant mount, which had originally held the two carved rubies. Since the sale in 1971, the necklace has once again been unmounted and the two large carved rubies, one depicting a dove and the other an angel, are now reunited as a pendant (p. 312).

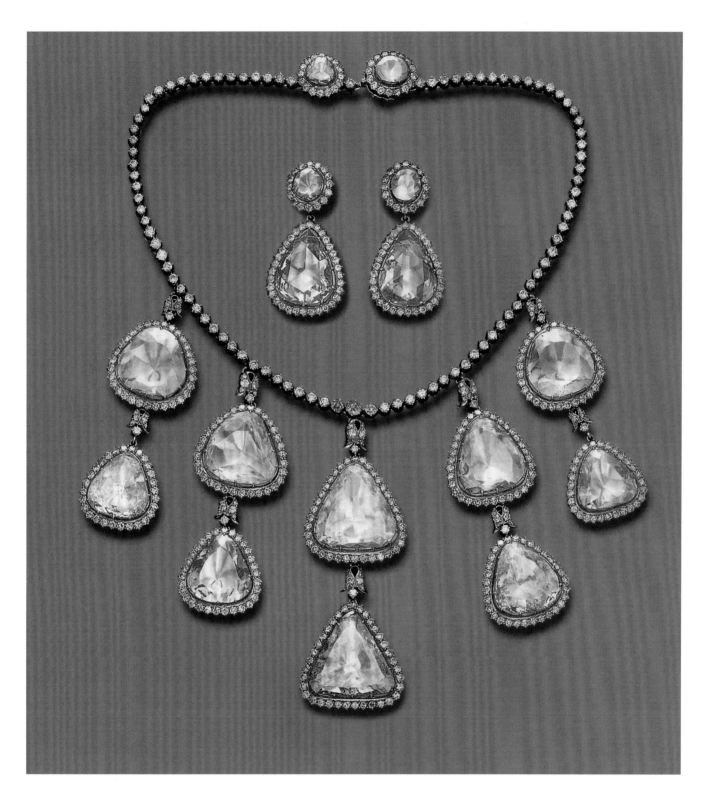

Opposite
A photograph from the Cartier, Paris archives of a diamond necklace by Cartier from 1931, set with ten large old Indian table-cut diamonds.

Above
The necklace as it appeared in the 1971 auction. By then it was a far less elaborate fringe necklace. Cartier Ltd; Sotheby's, New York (Parke-Bernet).

The cover of the 1971 sale catalogue was illustrated with a ruby and diamond butterfly brooch, the description noting that the body was set with a ruby of approximately 3.50 cts and a pear-shaped diamond, and that the four diamond wings were carved and mounted *en tremblant* (p. 288). What it failed to mention was that this remarkable jewel was created by Boucheron around 1894 and that the diamond wings were carved by C. Bordinckx, Frédéric Boucheron's well-known diamond cutter. Towards the end of the 19th century Bordinckx was already famous for his skilfully carved and executed diamond jewels, and the delicately lifelike veins on this butterfly's wings are a testament to his talent. There were also jewels by Seaman Schepps, the talented New York jeweler who created many fine sculptural pieces from the 1930s onwards and counted the likes of Coco Chanel and the Duchess of Windsor among his clients. Ganna acquired several jewels from him, including two large brooches, each a sunburst motif of looped goldwork decorated with brilliant-cut diamonds, one set at the centre with a cabochon emerald and the other with a baroque pearl, both probably dating from the 1940s. Among her other purchases was a gold and citrine bracelet with a matching ring, and a gold and cabochon ruby bangle, which in 1971 was sold with the oval gold frame, set with 26 baroque pearls, in which it had originally been mounted.

Ganna's collection also featured a highly dramatic group of gold, sapphire, ruby and emerald jewels dating from the late 1930s, reminiscent of those sported by the Duchess of Windsor. A large butterfly clip of ribbed textured gold was set with cabochon stones and came with a pair of bangles and a two-stone ring. It has the distinctive style of a Suzanne Belperron creation, as do the carved chalcedony bangle set with a star sapphire of around 125 cts, and a rock crystal ring with a star sapphire. A jewelry devotee such as Ganna would have appreciated the unique and innovative style of this great French designer.

The reference in Ganna's memoirs to time spent in St Petersburg during her first marriage is supported by two jewels from Fabergé. Both were types of vanity case, made in St Petersburg around 1900 by the master craftsmen Heinrich Wigström. One was a simple rectangular design decorated with blue guilloche enamel, the sides and thumbpiece set with rose- and cushion-shaped diamonds and inscribed on the top 'Ganna'.

Above
A pair of natural pearl and diamond pendent earrings; the diamond settings originally supported ruby drops and the tops were cabochon rubies. In their original form they had been a Cartier creation, but in the sale the rubies were mounted together with diamonds in a far less dramatic style.

Centre
A natural black-pearl and diamond ring, as worn opposite.

Below
The 21.15-ct heart-shaped diamond ring given to Ganna Walska by Alec Cochran in 1920.

Opposite
Ganna Walska, strikingly dressed, adorned with her favourite natural pearl jewels including a black-pearl and diamond ring, promotes her own perfume – a business venture that unfortunately failed.

Opposite and left
Virgin gold, cabochon emerald, ruby and sapphire *demi-parure* by Suzanne Belperron, made up of a large stylized butterfly brooch and spiral cuffs. The photograph on this page shows Ganna Walska wearing the brooch in New York, 1939.

Below left and right
Walska in Idaho, c. 1942, around the time she acquired the Californian estate that would become Lotusland. Her brooch, enlarged to the right, is a sunburst motif of looped goldwork and diamonds with a baroque pearl at the centre by Seaman Schepps.

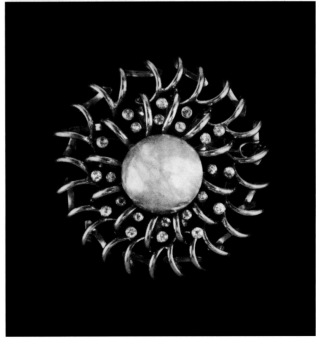

Above left
Two 19th-century carved rubies mounted as a pendant; the top stone shows a dove, the larger an angel at prayer. This modern setting adds a baroque pearl.

Above right
Ganna Walska wears the paired ruby pendant from long strings of ruby beads in the late 1930s. In her hand is the Boucheron butterfly brooch with diamond wings shown on page 288 and described on page 309.

Left
A flexible Art Deco bracelet in diamond and rock crystal, created by Cartier, Paris in 1930.

The interior contained the usual compartments for powder, rouge and lipstick. The other vanity case came in a more ingenious form: that of a parasol handle and vanity case combined. Again decorated with grey guilloche enamel and set with rose-cut diamonds, the hinged top opened to reveal a mirror and compartments for powder and lipstick. It is not known whether Ganna received these as gifts while in St Petersburg, if indeed she was there, or if they were bought as a reminder of her time in the city.

Ganna's collection was also remarkable for its extensive array of traditional Indian jewels, the majority of which she most certainly purchased from Cartier, whose archives recorded Indian jewels included in their stock since the 1870s. By the early years of the 20th century, Indian maharajahs were eager to have their jewels remounted in Europe by the master jewelers, while fashionable Europeans craved Indian jewels with their colourful enamel decoration and carved gemstones. These Indian jewels were also an important source of inspiration for European jewelers of the Art Deco period – especially Cartier, as can be seen in Ganna's collection. In 1911 Jacques Cartier made his first trip to India and he was quick to capitalize on the important opportunities, for both selling and buying, that this vast country offered. Hans Nadelhoffer noted that by the 1930s 'trendsetters like the Hon. Mrs Fellowes, Mrs Drexel Biddle, Ganna Walska and Mrs Harrison Williams spread the Indian fashion, which soon even the Duchess of Windsor was to take up.' Ganna's collection of over thirty Indian jewels included many bracelets, earrings and necklaces, one of the most spectacular examples being a suite of 19th-century jewelry from South India. The *parure* comprised a necklace, a bracelet and a pair of earrings set with rubies, emeralds and diamonds, and would have been worn by a traditional Indian dancer. There was also a 19th-century marriage necklace, possibly from Jaipur, as well as highly decorative bangles from Benares.

By the mid-1930s Ganna had finally bowed to public opinion and reluctantly given up her dream of becoming a great opera diva. She decided to spend most of her time at her château in France, where she continued to entertain the rich and famous and was easily persuaded to give impromptu recitals. Her attention now turned to mystics and gurus, much of her time occupied in searching for her true self and the 'meaning of life'. In the late 1930s she made a fifth marriage, to the English scientist Harry Grindell Matthews, followed in 1942 by a sixth, to the handsome 'White Lama' and yogi Theos Bernard, whom she met after attending one of his lectures.

At the outbreak of the Second World War, Ganna had returned to the United States, eventually settling in California with Bernard, and she remained there after his death in 1947. The sale of her jewels took place in New York in April 1971, when she was into her eighties. The reason she decided to part with all her remarkable jewels was to continue work on her dream project, a spectacular garden that she called 'Lotusland'. She had bought the property in California in 1941, hired Lockwood de Forest, a celebrated Santa Barbara landscape architect, to transform the grounds, and continued to reshape them for the rest of her life. The fabulous gardens are still admired in Lotusland today – a testament to her sense of beauty. The jewelry sale gave an insight into her remarkable collection and assured Ganna that even if she was not to be immortalized as a wonderful opera singer, she would surely be remembered as one of the great jewelry collectors of the 20th century. ✳

SELECTED BIBLIOGRAPHY

Aga Khan III, *The Memoirs of Aga Khan: World Enough and Time*, London, 1954

Arend, Liana Paredes, *French Furniture from the Collection of Hillwood Museum & Gardens*, Washington, D.C., 2006

Balfour, Ian, *Famous Diamonds*, London, 1987; 5th edn, Woodbridge, 2009

Beaton, Cecil, *The Glass of Fashion*, London, 1954

Bloch, Michael, *The Duchess of Windsor*, London, 1996

———, *The Reign and Abdication of Edward VIII*, London, 1990

——— (ed.), *Wallis and Edward: Letters 1931–37*, London, 1986

Cailles, Françoise, *René Boivin, Jeweller*, London, 1994

Cartier: Splendeurs de la Joaillerie, exh. cat., Lausanne, 1996

Celletti, Rodolfo, *Grandi voci alla Scala*, Milan, 1991

Coffin, Sarah D. and Suzy Menkes, *Set in Style: The Jewelry of Van Cleef & Arpels*, New York, 2010 and London, 2011

Cologni, Franco and Eric Nussbaum, *Platinum by Cartier: Triumphs of the Jewelers' Art*, New York, 1996

Corbett, Patricia, Ward Landrigan and Nico Landrigan, *Jewelry by Suzanne Belperron*, London and New York, 2016

Crespi Morbio, Vittoria, *Maria Callas: gli anni della Scala*, Turin, 2007

Culme, John and Nicholas Rayner, *The Jewels of the Duchess of Windsor*, London and New York, 1987

Dherbier, Yann-Brice, *Maria Callas*, Milan, 2009

Eldridge, Mona, *In Search of a Prince: My Life with Barbara Hutton*, London, 1988

Exhibition of Russian Art, 4 June–13 July 1935, exh. cat., London, 1935

Gardner II, Theodore Roosevelt, *Lotusland: A Photographic Odyssey*, Santa Barbara, 1995

Gatti, Carlo, *Il Teatro alla Scala nella storia e nell'arte, 1778–1958*, Milan, 1958

Hanine-Roussel, Jean-Jacques, *Callas Unica*, Chatou, 2002

Heymann, C. David, *Poor Little Rich Girl: The Life and Legend of Barbara Hutton*, London, 1985

Higham, Charles, *The Duchess of Windsor: The Secret Life*, New York, 1988; revd edn, 2004

——— and Roy Moseley, *Princess Merle, The Romantic Life of Merle Oberon*, New York, 1983

Hughes, Graham, *Modern Jewellery*, London, 1963

Jennings, Dean, *Barbara Hutton, A Candid Biography*, London and New York, 1968

Jutheau, Viviane, *Sterlé: Joaillier Paris*, Paris, 1990

Krashes, Laurence S., *Harry Winston, The Ultimate Jeweler*, 4th edn, New York, 1993

Levine, Robert, *Maria Callas: A Musical Biography*, New York, 2003

Menkes, Suzy, *The Royal Jewels*, London, 1985

———, *The Windsor Style*, London, 1987

Meylan, Vincent, *Archives secrètes Boucheron*, Paris, 2009

Nadelhoffer, Hans, *Cartier*, London and New York, 1984; revd edn, 2007

Néret, Gilles, *Boucheron: Four Generations of a World-Renowned Jeweler*, New York, 1988

Papi, Stefano and Alexandra Rhodes, *Famous Jewelry Collectors*, London, 1999

Pepper, Terence, *Dorothy Wilding: The Pursuit of Perfection*, London, 1991

Prior, Katherine and John Adamson, *Bijoux de Maharadjas*, Paris, 2000

Proddow, Penny and Debra Healy, *American Jewelry: Glamour and Tradition*, New York, 1987

——— and Marion Fase, *Hollywood Jewels: Movies, Jewelry, Stars*, New York, 1996

Pugliese, Giuseppe, *Herbert von Karajan: gli anni alla Scala*, Milan, 2000

Raulet, Sylvie, *Van Cleef & Arpels*, Paris and New York, 1986

Rochas, Sophie, *Marcel Rochas: Designing French Glamour*, Paris 2015

Rubin, Nancy, *American Empress: The Life and Times of Marjorie Merriweather Post*, New York, 1995

Rudoe, Judy, *Cartier: 1900–1939*, London and New York, 1997

———, 'Cartier in the nineteenth century', *Jewellery Studies*, vol. 9, London, 2001

Scarisbrick, Diana, *Chaumet: Master Jewellers Since 1780*, Woodbridge and Paris, 1995

Snowman, A. Kenneth (ed.), *The Master Jewelers*, London and New York, 1990; 2nd edn, 2002

Vickers, Hugo, *Behind Closed Doors: The Tragic, Untold Story of the Duchess of Windsor*, London, 2011

———, *Cecil Beaton: The Authorized Biography*, London, 1985

———, *The Private World of the Duke and Duchess of Windsor*, London, 1995

Walska, Ganna, *Always Room at the Top*, New York, 1943

Windsor, Edward, Duke of, *A King's Story: The Memoirs of HRH The Duke of Windsor*, London, 1951

Windsor, Wallis, Duchess of, *The Heart has its Reasons: The Memoirs of the Duchess of Windsor*, London, 1957

Youssoupoff, Félix, *Avant L'Exil: 1887–1919*, Paris, 1952

ACKNOWLEDGMENTS

We would especially like to thank the following:

HH Prince Amyn Aga Khan; Lilla Rowcliffe, daughter of Lydia, Lady Deterding, whose fascinating accounts of her mother's life helped to bring the chapter to life; the Comte de La Moussaye and Amoury de La Moussaye, the grandson and great-grandson of Daisy Fellowes; Cosimo Capanni; Carla Maria Casanova; Pauline Harding; Hannah Nepil; Zoe Rutherford; Mrs Judy Taubman; and Dario and Carlos Tettamanzi.

We are also grateful to friends and colleagues at the following companies, institutions and organizations:

Cartier: Michel Aliaga, Bernard Berger; Cecil Beaton Studio Archive, Sotheby's London: Joanna Ling and Katherine Marshall; Christie's, Geneva: Vanessa Cron; Christie's, London: Raymond Sancroft-Baker, Keith Penton; Forge & Lynch: Brendan Lynch; Getty Images: Luigi Didio; Hillwood Museum, Washington, DC: Liana Paredes, Audra Kelly, Marla DiVietro; The Mona Bismarck Foundation, Paris: Monica Dunham; Sotheby's Hong Kong: Chin Yeow Quek; Sotheby's London: Nathalie Rodwell, Jessica Wyndham, Don Franco Victor de Baux, Justin Roberts; Sotheby's Monte Carlo: Mark Armstrong; Sotheby's New York: Lisa Hubbard, Beth Wassarman, Carol Elkins; Van Cleef & Arpels: Catherine Cariou; Verdura: Ward and Nico Landrigan

At Thames & Hudson, we have been fortunate to work with a dedicated team, including Jamie Camplin, Helen Farr, Susanna Ingram, Julia MacKenzie and Niki Medlik. We would also like to express our appreciation of the book's designer, Carla Turchini, not only for her understanding of how we originally envisaged the book but also for being so enjoyable to work with.